JULIUS CAESAR

Also available or forthcoming in this series:

Augustine: The Confessions, Gillian Clark
Augustus: Caesar's Web: Power & Propaganda in Augustan Rome,
    Matthew Clark
Christian Martyrs and Ascetics, Aideen Hartney
Greek Tyranny, Sian Lewis
Hadrian's Wall, Geraint Osborn
Story & Spectacle: Rome at the Cinema, Elena Theodorakopoulos
The Greeks in Film and Popular Culture, Gideon Nisbet
The Politics of Greek Tragedy, David M. Carter
The Sword King: The Life & Legend of Leonidas of Thermopylae,
    Ian Macgregor Morris
The Trojan War, Emma Stafford

Julius Caesar in his prime

To Chris

JULIUS CAESAR

Robert Garland

*with warm wishes
on the occasion of your
visit to the Classics Dept.
Sept. 29, 06
Colgate U.*

BRISTOL PHOENIX PRESS

Cover illustration: *The Ides of March*, by Sir Edward John Poynter
© Manchester Art Gallery

First published in 2003 by
Bristol Phoenix Press
PO Box 2142
BRISTOL
BS99 7TS

© Robert Garland 2003

A catalogue record for this book is available
from the British Library.

ISBN 1-904675-02-6

Printed in Great Britain by
Booksprint

BRISTOL PHOENIX PRESS
Reed Hall • Streatham Drive
Exeter • EX4 4QR • UK
uep@exeterpress.co.uk • www.exeterpress.co.uk

For John Betts

But I wouldn't want <the years> back.
Not with the fire in me now.
No, I wouldn't want them back.

  [Samuel Beckett, *Krapp's Last Tape*]

Contents

Illustrations		ix
Preface		xi
Acknowledgements		xiii
Chronology		xiv
1	The Man	1
2	The Witnesses	7
3	The Crisis	13
4	The Ambitious Upstart	23
5	The Proconsul of Gaul	35
6	The Gambler	45
7	The Final Months	57
8	The Conspiracy	63
9	The Murder	71
10	The Funeral	81
11	The Avenger	87
12	The Legacy	95
13	The Verdict	99
14	The Media	105
Notes		115
Further Reading		119
Index		123

Illustrations

Figures

Fig. 1   The Julian Forum, bird's eye view [based on the reconstruction in Museo della Civiltà Romana, Rome]   4

Fig. 2   Map of Italy [drawn by Myongsun Kong, Colgate University]   12

Fig. 3   Map of the Roman empire [drawn by Myongsun Kong, Colgate University]   15

Fig. 4   Gladiatorial combat at a Roman funeral [from *The Antiquities of Rome* by Basil Kennett, 1721]   28

Fig. 5   The Roman Forum *ca* 50 BCE, plan [from *Cicero* by Anthony Everitt © 2002; by permission of Random House Inc.]   30

Fig. 6   Map of Gaul [drawn by Myongsun Kong, Colgate University   37

Fig. 7   The Roman Forum *ca* 50 BCE, reconstruction [from *The Ancient Roman City* by John E. Stambaugh © 1988; by permission of Johns Hopkins University Press]   53

Fig. 8   The theatre and colonnade of Pompey, bird's eye view [based on the reconstruction in Museo della Civiltà Romana, Rome]   73

Plates

Frontispiece C. Julius Caesar, portrait bust [Museo Campo Santo, Pisa; by permission of the Ministero per Ì Beni e le Attività, Culturali]   *facing p.* vii

Plate i   C. Julius Caesar, portrait bust [Turin Museum; by permission Ministero per Ì Beni e le Attività Culturali]   4

Plate ii   Cn. Pompeius Magnus, portrait bust [Ny Carlsberg Glyptothek, Copenhagen; by permission]   5

Plate iii   M. Tullius Cicero, portrait bust [Apsley House, London; by permission of the Victoria and Albert Museum]   8

Plate iv   [?] C. Cassius Longinus, portrait bust [Museum of Fine Arts, Montreal; by permission]   9

Plate v   M. Antonius, portrait bust [Kingston Lacey, Dorset; by permission National Trust Photo Library, Paul Mulcahy]   66

Plate vi   Coins of (a) C. Julius Caesar [by permission of the Trustees of the British Museum]; (b) M. Antonius [from *Horace in his Odes* by J. Harrison; by permission of Gerald Duckworth & Co Ltd]; (c) Cleopatra VII   *facing p.* 67

Plate vii   C. Octavius, later Octavianus, portrait bust [by permission Musée de l'Arles antique, Cl.M. Lacanaud]   88

Plate viii   Coins of (a) M. Junius Brutus, obverse (b) reverse (c) Cn. Pompeius Magnus [by permission of the Trustees of the British Museum]   89

Plate ix   (a) Willam Warren as Caesar in *Cleopatra,* Paramount Pictures, 1934 (b) Louis Cahern as Caesar in the film of Shakespeare's *Julius Caesar*, MGM, 1953 [courtesy of the British Film Institute, Stills Department]   108

Plate x   Claude Rains as Caesar in the film of G.B. Shaw's *Caesar and Cleopatra*, MGM, 1946 [courtesy of the British Film Institute, Stills Department]   109

Plate xi   (a) Rex Harrison as Caesar and Elizabeth Taylor as Cleopatra in *Cleopatra*, Twentieth-Century-Fox, 1963 (b) Astérix with Cleopatra in the film *Astérix et Cléopâtra*, Dargaud-Marina, 1968 [courtesy of the British film Institute, Stills Department]   110

Plate xii   Rex Harrison as Caesar discovering Cleopatra in the carpet in *Cleopatra*, Twentieth Century Fox, 1963 [courtesy of the British Film Institute, Stills Department]   111

Preface

Julius Caesar is, quite simply, the most famous Roman who ever lived. Practically everyone knows that he was an epileptic; that he conquered Gaul; that he invaded Britain; that he initiated a civil war by crossing the River Rubicon and saying, 'The die is cast'; that he had an affair with Cleopatra, queen of Egypt, who had herself delivered to him inside a carpet; that he was murdered on the ides of March; and that his dying words were – according to Shakespeare – '*Et tu, Brute*'.

But do these 'facts' provide the true explanation for his fame? Is there, in other words, an explanation under the explanation? From antiquity onwards Caesar has exercised a fascination over historians, over philosophers, and, in more recent times, over playwrights, opera composers, novelists and film-directors. Is this due to the 'facts' or is it perhaps due to his energy, his versatility, his generalship, his intellect, his will, his daring, his courage, his ambition, his tenacious grip on power, his audacious fatalism, his much-tested magnanimity, his influence upon the future course of Roman history, his impact upon the creation of Europe, his legacy of the Julian calendar, or the terrifying nature of his death – stabbed by his closest political allies as well as by his pardoned enemies? All of the above, I would argue, play their part.

There is another question. If, as seems inevitable, Caesar's hold over the western imagination proves to be eternal, does that justify us in regarding him as 'great'? What, after all, is this thing we call 'greatness', and can it aptly be applied to a man whose character was vitiated by a number of serious flaws – one, moreover, who initiated a civil war to safeguard his own interests, was responsible for the deaths of perhaps over a million human beings, many of them his fellow citizens, and who aroused as much fear and loathing among his peers as any man who ever lived?

Finally, historians are increasingly coming to the realisation that the history of the reception of events and lives, as well as of works of art, constitutes an essential element in how we perceive previous periods of history and their products. For this reason the last two chapters of this book examine Caesar's legacy, his importance within the western intellectual tradition, and his depiction in a variety of media.

Abbreviations

Appian *CW* = *Civil Wars*
Caesar *CW* = *Commentaries on the Civil War*
Caesar *GW* = *Commentaries on the Gallic Wars*
Cassius Dio *RH* = *Roman History*
Lucan *CW* = *Civil War*
Plutarch *JC* = *Julius Caesar*
Suetonius *DJ* = *Divus* ('divine') *Julius*
Velleius Paterculus *RH* = *Roman Histories*

For standard abbreviations of Roman personal names, see note 1 (p. 115).
All dates given are BCE, unless specifically stated to be CE.

Acknowledgements

I wish to thank John Betts and John North, who read versions of this book at different stages and made invaluable suggestions. John North stepped in at a late stage and disabused me of many errors in several of the early chapters. All remaining faults are mine and I gladly take responsibility for them. I also wish to thank Jean Scott, who proof-read the manuscript with an attentive ear to cadence as well as a sharp eye to orthography.

Acknowledgements for use of illustrations appear with the list on pages ix-x; every effort has been made to acquire permissions, to render the list as full as possible. Any organisation claiming copyright may contact the publisher.

Chronology

100   Born on 13th July

84   Marries Cornelia, daughter of Cinna

80   Serves under the governor of Asia and wins military decoration; alleged affair with Nicomedes IV of Bithynia

81   Birth of his daughter Julia

75   Captured by pirates

73   Minor pontiff

72   Military tribune

67   Marries Pompeia, Sulla's grand-daughter

65   Curule aedile

63   Supreme pontiff

62   Praetor; divorces Pompeia

61   Proconsul of Further Spain

60   Forms 'triumvirate' with Pompey and Crassus

59   First consulship; marries Calpurnia; Pompey marries Julia

58   Proconsul of Gaul

56   'Triumvirate' is renewed

55   Caesar's proconsulship is prolonged for five years; he bridges the Rhine; first expedition to Britain

54   Second expedition to Britain; death of Julia

52   Caesar suppresses revolt of Vercingetorix at Alesia; campaigns in absentia for consulship

51   End of Gallic War; Caesar publishes seven books of *Commentaries* on the Gallic War

49   Crosses the Rubicon on 10th January and initiates the Civil War; Pompeian forces in Spain surrender; elected dictator

48   Second consulship; resigns dictatorship; defeats Pompey at Pharsalus; occupies Alexandria; meets Cleopatra

47   Elected dictator for a year; installs Cleopatra as queen of Egypt; defeats Pharnaces at Zela in Asia Minor

46   Third consulship; defeats Pompeians at Thapsus in Africa; elected dictator for ten years

45   Fourth consulship; defeats Pompey's sons at Munda; end of Civil War; celebrates quadruple triumph; elected dictator for life

Chapter 1
The Man

Gaius[1] Julius Caesar is described in the literary sources as tall, with a
pale complexion, shapely limbs, a rather chubby face and black, piercing
eyes. (We should bear in mind that 'tall' for a Roman was perhaps a mere
5'6" [1.78m.].) We also have six portraits in marble, thought to have
been executed in his lifetime. One of the best of the later years, a head in
Turin (pl. i), depicts a balding man with a large brow, prominent nose and
long, scraggy neck. A sardonic smile plays around his lips.

Though he was not particularly robust, his capacity for physical
endurance was formidable. He often marched alongside his legionaries,
bareheaded in both sun and rain, and made it a point of honour to endure the
same hardships. He was phenomenally strong and sometimes manhandled
his soldiers, grabbing them by the throat to prevent them from turning to
flight. On one occasion he is said to have swum two hundred yards using
only one arm in order to prevent the documents he was holding in the other
from getting wet, while dragging his tunic in his teeth so that the enemy
would not seize it as booty. He was an excellent horseman and could
gallop at top speed with his hands behind his back. Towards the end of his
life he suffered increasingly from epilepsy, an illness that was thought to
provide evidence in the victim of divine favour. Interestingly, the Latin for
'epilepsy' (*morbus comitalis*) translates as the 'disease relating to public
meetings' because an attack, which was regarded as a sign from the gods,
justified the postponement of a public meeting.

Caesar's legionaries mocked him for being a womaniser and a
sodomite, though this is the kind of allegation that legionaries would
make to vaunt their general's sexual prowess. 'The bald whoremonger'
is how they described him, while C. Scribonius Curio, at first Caesar's
opponent but later his ally, referred to him in public as 'every woman's
man and every man's woman.' (Suetonius *DJ* 52.3). Like most Romans,
he probably consorted frequently with slaves and prostitutes, particularly
when on campaign. It is no doubt because this practice was commonplace
that our sources say nothing about it, other than the fact that he spent a
vast sum of money acquiring comely slaves. Suetonius' list (*DJ* 50-52) of

1

his sexual conquests, which includes the wives of his two closest political associates, reminds one of Henry Kissinger's famous observation that 'power is the ultimate aphrodisiac'. The list should, however, be treated with extreme caution, partly because it may have been concocted by his enemies to tarnish his reputation. However, there is every likelihood that Caesar was over-sexed; and one cannot help wondering how many of his assassins might also have been his cuckolds. Apart from the fact that he had a youthful affair with king Nicomedes of Bithynia, there is no evidence that he had any homosexual inclinations. Not even his enemies were able to link him erotically to any other man.

Caesar's most passionate romance is said to have been with Servilia, the mother of the assassin M. Junius Brutus. Although he refused a request by the dictator L. Cornelius Sulla to divorce his first wife Cornelia, this may have been because he considered it an insult rather than evidence of deep affection. He readily divorced his second wife Pompeia when an allegation of adultery was made against her, and that without establishing the facts behind the case. He also offered to divorce Calpurnia, his wife of a few months, for the sake of a political alliance with Pompeius Magnus (Pompey [pl. ii]). We know of no-one to whom Caesar opened his heart, though Cleopatra, with whom he had a notorious affair towards the end of his life, probably came closest to being a soul-mate.

He was a connoisseur of gem stones, luxury vases and old paintings, on which he expended vast sums of money. At a time when he was heavily in debt, he bought Servilia a pearl costing 60,000 gold *denarii*[2], perhaps in part to demonstrate to the world his unshakeable confidence in his own prospects. He built an expensive villa on lake Nemi in Latium and had it pulled down soon afterwards because it failed to satisfy his taste. There is no record of what he paid in bribes, though he owed one of his creditors alone 36 million sesterces. Even his enemies conceded that he was abstemious in regard to food and drink. M. Porcius Cato, who hated him with a passion, wryly observed that Caesar was the only man who tried to overthrow the constitution when sober.

Though he was an outstanding general, he was nonetheless capable of committing major tactical errors. The success of his Gallic campaign in particular was jeopardised by his invasion of Britain. He was fully aware of the part that chance (*fortuna*) played in war. He earned an unrivalled reputation for *celeritas*, 'rapidity', requiring his men to make forced marches even when they served no practical purpose. More than once he snatched victory from the jaws of defeat by his daredevil courage. He was indifferent to death and on many occasions recklessly risked his life in battle. A few weeks before his assassination he dismissed his Spanish bodyguard, declaring that it was 'better to die once than always to be fearing death' (Plutarch *JC* 57.4).

He was gifted with prodigious powers of concentration, being capable according to Pliny (*Natural History* 7.91) of simultaneously dictating four different letters to four different secretaries. He had a natural gift for oratory, pronouncing in a high-pitched voice and using lively movements and gestures. Cicero (*Brutus* 261) described him as 'a master of a type of eloquence that is brilliant though unstudied, which in respect of his voice, gestures and whole physique exhibits a certain noble and high-bred quality'. He was a gifted and versatile writer. Though only his *Commentaries* have survived, he also wrote two books on grammatical analogy, a poem called 'The Journey', and a book of jokes and *bon mots*. Most of these were produced while he was on campaign. He was a copious pamphleteer and an indefatigable correspondent. He possessed a subtle and penetrating intellect, and had an unrivalled flare for politics. Even so, he was capable of allowing his emotions to cloud his better judgment, as when he represented his victories over Pompey's supporters in Egypt and Spain as triumphs over a foreign enemy.

Despite being head of the college of pontiffs (*pontifex maximus* – a title of uncertain origin meaning 'chief-bridge-maker'), Caesar probably did not believe in the gods – at least not in the gods as they were conventionally conceived by the Romans of his time. Indisputably he employed religion for his own aggrandisement. He was distrustful of portents, or at least of their conventional interpretation, though we should be wary of labelling him a cynical manipulator of religious sentiment. On the other hand, he would not have achieved all he did without adhering to the firm conviction that he was a man marked out by destiny. Another way of putting this would be to say that he was endowed with boundless optimism: a man capable of mesmerising himself by the plausibility of his own argumentation and the force of his own convictions.

In forming an estimate of Caesar's character, we need to distinguish between what our sources tell us (not necessarily accurate) and what modern historians infer (obviously suppositious). It is alleged that he was vain but this is precisely the kind of trivial criticism that is likely to have been levelled at him by his enemies, who were evidently hard-pressed to cite more serious character flaws. As *pontifex maximus*, Caesar had the exclusive right to wear a crimson *toga*[3]; he apparently drew further attention to himself by wearing a loose-fitting belt. He is said to have used tweezers to remove his pubic hairs and to have been preoccupied with his baldness, which he attempted to disguise by combing his hair forward from the crown of his head (Suetonius *DJ* 45.2). To suggest that he made light of the distinctions awarded him by the senate, his enemies claimed that his favourite honour was the right to wear a laurel wreath on any occasion he chose, since this concealed his 'disfigurement' entirely.

He was a classic type-A personality – a workaholic, as we would call him today. He was intensely aggressive and competitive, particularly when it came to Pompey, his rival for power in the Civil War and probably the only man among his contemporaries with whom he deigned to compare himself (pl. ii). If Pompey celebrated a triple triumph, Caesar must celebrate a quadruple one. If Pompey built a stone theatre, Caesar must outdo him by building another in stone, as well as refurbishing the forum and adding an extension, which he named the Julian Forum after

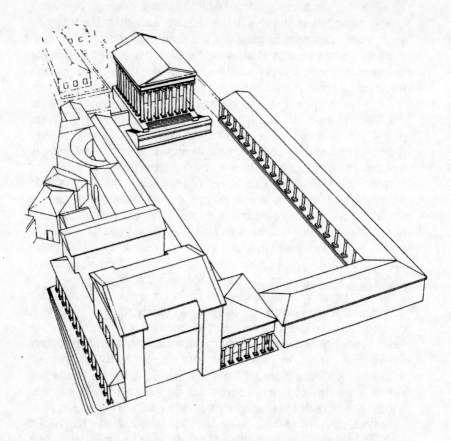

Fig. 1 The Julian Forum dominated by the temple of Venus Genetrix, bird's eye view

Plate i. Julius Caesar in old age

597
POMPEJUS MAGNUS
d. 48 f. Kr.

Plate ii.   Pompey

his own Julian clan or *gens*. Similarly, if Cicero wrote a pamphlet praising Caesar's dead enemy Cato, he had to respond by writing an 'Anti-Cato' to set the record straight (see p. 51). He never compromised on a point of honour and he never ducked a fight. He had a genius for presenting his enemies in an unfavourable light and for representing their opposition to him as a breach of the law that could only to be rectified by force.

He must have been enormously charismatic and, to put it crudely, a deft schmoozer – highly adept at working the crowd. As the outpouring of grief at his funeral makes clear, he won the hearts of thousands. He achieved this in part by cultivating his public image and by expert manipulation of the instruments of propaganda, by spin. To his social inferiors, including his legionaries and the urban poor, he was Mr Affability. To those who posed a threat or merely a challenge to his ambition, he was domineering, disdainful and aloof. Cicero, who entertained him at his country estate a few months before his death, revealingly observed (*Letters to Atticus* 13.52) that 'he was not the kind of guest to whom you say, "come over next time you're in the neighbourhood". Once is enough.' At the same time he was a loyal and faithful friend. When Cicero's daughter Tullia died in childbirth, he found time on his way back from Spain to write a touching letter of consolation, even though he was at the time nursing a grudge against Cicero for having published a defence of Cato.

There is nothing to support Cicero's claim (*de officiis* [*on Duties*] 2.84) that 'his passion for wrongdoing was so great that the very doing of wrong was a joy for its own sake, even when there was no motive for it'. Though he acted at times with appalling cruelty, he was prepared to come to terms with his bitterest foes. In fact he made a veritable cult of his *clementia* (clemency). This quality probably derived from a generous nature, a consciousness of his own innate superiority, a lofty contempt for punishment as a means to a political end and a determination not to repeat the faults of Sulla, who had acted with brutal vindictiveness towards his enemies (see p. 13). At the same time it was a valuable political tool, which he exploited to undermine resistance and opposition. In other ways Caesar used Sulla as his model: his own career would not have taken the course it did, had not Sulla blazed the trail before him; like Sulla, Caesar marched on Rome; like Sulla, Caesar initiated a civil war; and like Sulla he was proclaimed *dictator perpetuo* (dictator in perpetuity).

Caesar possessed enormous strength of will. His self-sufficiency, as we might call it, probably exceeded that of any other man of his generation. His energy was phenomenal and he never rested on his laurels, to coin a phrase. In Lucan's words Caesar 'thought nothing was done so long as anything remained to be done' (*CW* 2.657). He was reticent about his true feelings and the quality of his inner life escapes us entirely. Quite possibly the only human being whom he ever really loved was his daughter Julia. It goes without saying that he had a giant-sized ego, bolstered by his conviction of righteous destiny. As he openly proclaimed at the outbreak of the Civil War, his *dignitas* (public standing) was dearer than life itself (*CW* 1.7). In his final months he became morbidly obsessed with the respect that he had earned from the Roman establishment. Though outwardly he gives the impression of being ice-cool in the face of every challenge, it is all too easy to read his career as a *fait accompli* from start to finish. It certainly was not and there must have been times, particularly during the Gallic revolt and the Civil War, when he was downcast, perhaps even depressed.

Caesar stood for no cause. It is not recorded whether he had a conscience nor whether in his darkest moments he ever agonised over the multitude of sufferings he inflicted upon his countrymen, not to mention upon other races, but the likelihood is that a moral vacuum lay at the core of his being. As much as any man who ever lived he gave paramountcy to self-interest.

On the day of his death he was surely one of the loneliest men alive.

Chapter 2

The Witnesses

Julius Caesar aroused contrasting passions of hatred and admiration in all who knew him, and it is inevitable that this should be reflected in our testimonies – all the more so given the circumstances of his death, which prompted a propagandist war between his assassins and his supporters. Even so, we should not naively assume that any one surviving account of Caesar's life is simplistically *either* friendly *or* hostile. All in their different ways may be coloured by both traditions. For these reasons the attempt to arrive at a balanced assessment of Caesar's career is a difficult undertaking, made yet more challenging by the strong feelings which it continues to arouse today. A particularly interesting feature of the tradition is the preservation of an unusually large number of quotations attributed to him.

Caesar was assassinated because he was bent on destroying the Republic and setting up a *regnum* (kingship) in its place. Or at least that is the point of view of the hostile testimony, which sought to prove that he coveted despotism from very early in his career. The friendly testimony sought to establish that he had no such designs even at the end of his life. There was, however, a complication in that Caesar's grand-nephew C. Octavius, who later became the emperor Augustus, owed his rise to power largely to Caesar's adoption of him by the terms of his will (see p. 51). When he first came to prominence, the young Octavius would have needed to promote a positive image of his grand-uncle in order to counter the suggestion that his adoptive father was a tyrant, which is what the assassins maintained. When Octavius became emperor, however, Caesar's legacy would have become a liability to him, as he sought to establish a disguised monarchy. Consequently, he would have needed to distance himself from Caesar's career for fear of inviting a similar fate. At a deeper level he may even have secretly sympathised with the assassins. At all accounts it was not in his interests to expunge all negative bias from the record.

Our chief witness for Caesar's military accomplishments is Caesar himself, whose seven books of *Commentaries on the Gallic War* (*de*

7

bello Gallico) relate the events of his proconsulship of Gaul from 58 to 52. Somewhat to the detriment of their popularity, these were for a long time the standard Latin works to which elementary language students were first introduced (a tradition that began in the sixteenth century), since their author was a stickler for grammar and made use of a very restricted vocabulary (only 1300 words in all). The *Commentaries* were much admired in antiquity. Cicero, for instance, praised them for being 'unadorned, direct and graceful' (Suetonius *DJ* 56). An eighth book, written by Aulus Hirtius, his secretary in Gaul, covers the final two years of the war.

In order to give his account the appearance of objectivity, and perhaps as well to drain it of emotion, Caesar almost invariably refers to himself in the third person. He never discloses to his readers the grand design, which was to bring the whole of free Gaul under his control. Instead he presents himself as a model governor, rapidly traversing the province to defend Rome's allies and reinforce her national security. He thus presents his conquest as the gradual overcoming of a series of local difficulties. The *Commentaries* are quite simply a masterpiece of narratological understatement and deception.

Although it was Caesar's intention to impress upon his readership the invaluable services which he had rendered to the state, the essential accuracy of his account is accepted by most scholars. Probably none, however, would claim him to be entirely innocent of misrepresentation. Written at the end of each year's campaigning, the *Commentaries* are widely regarded as models of military history, though there are some highly revealing omissions. Some of these omissions reflect Caesar's propagandist goal, while others are indicative of his idiosyncratic style of leadership. For instance, he tells us little about his senior staff (*legati* or legates) and we are left with the distinct impression that he rarely consulted them. Similarly he gives them little credit for his military successes. Even Q. Atius Labienus, his second-in-command for most of the Gallic War, plays a very minor role in the narrative. When an initiative of particular daring on the part of Labienus leads to the suppression of an insurrection, all that Caesar manages to come up with is, 'fortune approved Labienus' strategy' (*GW* 5.58). Labienus deserted to Pompey in the Civil War, and it may be that there was already some animosity between him and Caesar. Of the common soldiery the only ones referred to by name are his centurions and standard-bearers, who receive honorable mention for acts of bravery. Nor does he provide much information about such crucial matters as the stocking of the quartermaster's stores, the work of his medical orderlies or the labours of his engineers. Very rarely does

Plate iii. Cicero

Plate iv.   Cassius (probably)

he acknowledge a military failure and never once does he assume full responsibility for it. A conspicuous example is to be found in his account of the invasion of Britain, which on more than one occasion nearly turned into a disaster. Thus, when describing the abortive landing on the island in 55, he states that 'Caesar's previous good fortune was found lacking' (*GW* 4.26). What he fails to admit, here or anywhere else, is that Caesar screwed up.

Caesar's three books of *Commentaries on the Civil War* (*de bello civili*) detail his subsequent struggle with Pompey. For reasons which are unclear, he abandoned his narrative shortly after Pompey's death. It was continued in three further books, generally referred to as *Commentaries on the African, Alexandrian* and *Spanish Wars* respectively, by unknown authors. They were published the year after Caesar's death, largely, we suspect, in order to vindicate him posthumously against the charge of tyrannical behaviour. Their effect on public opinion is impossible to judge.

The other important contemporary source is to be found in the letters of the celebrated orator and politician, M. Tullius Cicero (pl. iii). As Cicero was an old friend of Caesar but a partisan of Pompey, his relationship with Caesar was extremely conflicted. Though not privy to the murder plot, he certainly fanned the flames of hatred against the dictator, whose domination offended him deeply. Cicero corresponded not only with Caesar but also with many of his enemies, in whom he regularly confided his fears. He has often been accused of hypocrisy in his dealings with Caesar but the truth is that his position was an extremely awkward one. His letters, which were not published until the first century CE, have come down to us in two main collections entitled *Letters to Friends* and *Letters to Atticus*. They provide invaluable testimony regarding Caesar's dwindling popularity at the end of his life. Cicero is also an important witness for the period immediately after the murder, when he reflects, sometimes in correspondence with M. Brutus, C. Cassius (pl. iv) and other conspirators, upon their failure to grasp the political initiative.

Other contemporary sources include the historian Sallust, who in a monograph entitled *The War Against Catiline* (*bellum Catilinae*) describes Caesar's involvement with the Catilinarian conspiracy of 63 (p. 29 f.). The poet Catullus, more famed for his love poetry, wrote a few scurrilous verses about Caesar, which deeply offended him though he took no action against their author. We also have an account of the murder in a fragmentary biography of Augustus written in Greek by Nicolaus of Damascus. Nicolaus drew on Augustus' now-lost autobiography and his account is fulsome in its praise of the emperor. A biography by C. Oppius,

Caesar's agent and confidant, is no longer extant. Also lost is C. Asinius Pollio's *History*, which began with the compact between Caesar, Pompey and M. Crassus in 60 (the so-called 'first triumvirate') and terminated with the battle of Philippi in 42. The work was used by both Plutarch and Appian (see below). In view of the fact that Pollio, a Republican of the old school, resisted pressure from Augustus to conform to the ideals of the new imperial era, the loss of his work is particularly regrettable. We also lack the accounts of a number of hostile contemporary witnesses who charged Caesar – totally preposterously – with plotting to overthrow the Republic in the mid-60's. It is tempting but tendentious to suspect that their testimonies were suppressed.

All our other sources postdate Caesar's death by at least two generations. The earliest is Velleius Paterculus, who wrote a lacklustre *Compendium of Roman History*, which is viewed with contempt by some scholars because of its favourable attitude to both Caesar and to the Julio-Claudian dynasty established by Augustus. Lucan's epic poem *The Civil War* (*bellum civile*) narrates the power struggle between Pompey and Caesar. Though Lucan, who lived in the time of the emperor Nero, falsifies facts for his own dramatic purposes, his work has much to tell us about how Caesar's reputation was faring in the middle of the first century CE. An encyclopaedic compilation of fascinating trivia in thirty-one books entitled *Natural History* by Pliny the Elder preserves a few interesting anecdotes about Caesar.

Our two surviving biographies were compiled well over a century after Caesar's death. The earlier is by Plutarch, a Greek philosopher whose *Parallel Lives* paired famous Greek politicians and soldiers with their Roman counterparts. (Caesar was paired with Alexander the Great.) Plutarch read widely and occasionally quotes his sources, though he uses them somewhat uncritically. Although his writing is not particularly profound or illuminating, he distils his biographical accounts into a succession of dramatic gestures and memorable words with an emphasis upon *êthos*, the moral essence of his subjects' personality. While making no secret of the fact that what cost Caesar his life was his passion to be king, he gives full credit to many of his positive attributes, including his clemency, his yearning for military glory, his disdain for death, his courage and his leadership. Plutarch also wrote biographies of other leading late-Republican figures in Caesar's circle including Mark Antony, Marcus Brutus, Cicero and Pompey.

Plutarch's younger contemporary Suetonius wrote a biography of *The Divine Julius* (*divus Julius*) which incorporates considerable backstairs gossip, much of it scurrilous. He should not, however, be dismissed simply as a scandal-monger. Suetonius served for a time as secretary to the emperor Hadrian and had access to the imperial archives. He presents a more vivid and psychologically rounded picture of his subject than Plutarch, devoting much attention to personal details, but is not entirely trustworthy. Suetonius shows much interest in Caesar's sex life – a topic ignored by Plutarch, perhaps because he considered it inappropriate in a historical account. Though more critical than Plutarch, he also stresses Caesar's good qualities as well as his defects: for instance, he speaks approvingly of Caesar's abstemiousness, his powers of endurance, and his leadership; disparagingly of his dishonesty in money matters, and his lack of religious scruples. Uniquely among ancient writers Suetonius castigates Caesar for his wanton destructiveness, claiming that he laid waste towns merely for the sake of plunder rather than because of any misconduct on the part of their inhabitants. He shows little interest in politics or war; and he devotes only one paragraph to the entirety of the Gallic Wars. Though he does not attribute to Caesar any long-term plan to acquire sole power, Suetonius concludes that he deserved assassination because of the excessive honours which he accepted in the final months of his life.

We also have two general accounts of the late Republic, both written in Greek. The earlier is by Appian (first half of the second century CE), whose history of the *Civil Wars* (*bellum civile*) is pro-republican. Much of Appian's material is derived from recent imperial writers. The later is by Cassius Dio (late second or early third century CE), whose *Roman History* (*Historiae Romanae*) is adulatory.

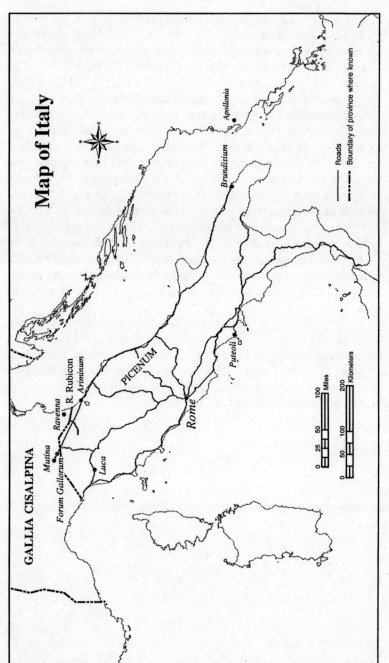

Fig. 2

Chapter 3

The Crisis

Caesar's birth, probably in the year 100 BCE, occurred at a time of increasing conflict and civil disturbance. When he was twelve, an ambitious general named Cornelius Sulla Felix turned his legions against Rome. When he was eighteen, a bloody civil war broke out. The war lasted sporadically for six years and ended in Sulla's favour. In the course of it Sulla all but annihilated a warlike Italian people known as the Samnites, who inhabited the central southern Apennines. At its conclusion he proscribed (posted in public places) the names of all his political enemies. They were deemed to be outlaws and could be killed with impunity. Though ancient sources put the figure as high as 6,000, it is estimated that about 520 perished in this way. The state confiscated their property, which was auctioned off at knockdown prices. A year later Sulla was elected dictator and attempted to restore normal constitutional procedures. Two years later, possibly because of failing health, he resigned his post and retired from public life.

These events must have left an indelible impression on Caesar, not least by proving to him that an ambitious politician could achieve anything so long as he was convinced of the rightness of his cause and was prepared to back up his conviction with force. Caesar's career should therefore be judged against a background of vicious political in-fighting the like of which has scarcely been equalled in any so-called civilized society.

The *respublica* ('commonwealth' is probably the closest translation, though 'republic' is generally preferred) had stood the test of time for nearly half a millennium. It had come into being following the expulsion of Tarquinius Superbus (Tarquin the Proud), the last king of Rome, in 510. It was founded on an entrenched fear of autocratic power, since the very word *rex*'(king) was synonymous with every Roman's worst nightmare. The Republic was designed to restrict the amount of power that any single individual could wield by means of a sophisticated system of checks and balances. In Caesar's day, however, it was coming under increasing strain, largely due to the fact that it could no longer cope with the administration of Rome's vast Mediterranean-based empire (fig. 3). In fact it is fair to say that many of the abuses that were committed by powerful individuals like Sulla and Caesar were 'structural'; that is to say, independent of the characters involved, and the consequence of Rome's success in foreign policy.

The crisis of the late Republic took a variety of forms. To begin with, there were deep-seated problems in Rome's governing body, the senate. From Sulla onwards the senate comprised 600 magistrates and ex-magistrates, all of whom had at least to have been appointed to the quaestorship (see next page). Although the popular assemblies elected all the magistrates, the senate was a highly exclusive body, rather like an old boys' club, since entry was very much dependent upon birth. From the end of the second century, however, *novi homines* or 'new men', belonging to families which had never previously been represented, had occasionally been appointed. The most distinguished of these were C. Marius and, a generation later, Cicero, both of whom rose to the rank of *consul*, even though their ancestors had not held any magistracies. Interestingly, too, both men came from Arpinum (modern Arpino). In theory the senate had no formal powers and its decrees had to be ratifed by the people to become law. In practice it was consulted by Roman magistrates in the performance of all but the most routine of their duties and those who ignored its recommendations did so at their peril. It supervised legislation, controlled expenditure, directed foreign policy, organised conquered territories, allocated military commands, and voted troops and supplies to generals in the field. In times of emergency it passed the *senatus consultum ultimum* (last decree of the senate), instructing the consuls 'to see that the Republic suffer no harm'.

From the late second century the influence and authority of the senate were consistently undermined, first in domestic policy and later in foreign policy, primarily by demagogic tribunes of the *plebs* (common people – see below). The pioneer in this movement was Ti. Sempronius Gracchus who, as tribune in 133, introduced a proposal distributing land to the poor. Sulla sought to shore up the senate's powers by introducing a variety of constitutional reforms. Less than a decade after his death most of them had been swept away by Pompey and M. Licinius Crassus, his one-time allies. The senate's independence and standing reached rock bottom in the months leading up to Caesar's death, when all it could do was rack its collective brains to devise ever more grandiose honours to bestow upon him. It never regained its former prestige, though the emperors preserved the fiction that it remained an important consultative body.

A further problem was that ambitious politicians like Pompey broke the rules which had been laid down for the advancement of magistrates.

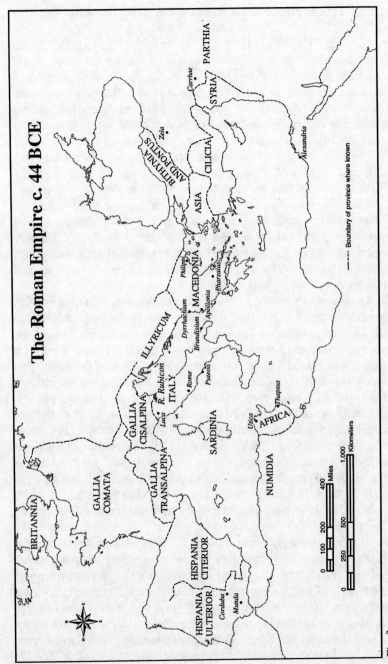

The Roman Empire c. 44 BCE

BRITANNIA

GALLIA COMATA

GALLIA CISALPINA

GALLIA TRANSALPINA

ITALY

ILLYRICUM

Luca

R. Rubicon

Rome

Puteoli

SARDINIA

HISPANIA CITERIOR

HISPANIA ULTERIOR

Corduba

Munda

NUMIDIA

AFRICA

Utica

Thapsus

Brundisium

Dyrrhachium

Apollonia

MACEDONIA

Philippi

Pharsalus

ASIA

BITHYNIA AND PONTUS

Zela

CILICIA

SYRIA

PARTHIA

Carrhae

Alexandria

Miles

0   100   200   400

Kilometers

0   250   500   1,000

– – – – Boundary of province where known

Fig. 3

(Caesar's rise to prominence was, by contrast, fairly orthodox). From the early second century onwards a law had been in place to regulate the steps in the so-called ladder of offices (*cursus honorum*) which a politician had to ascend in order to progress from a junior to a senior magistracy. Later minimum age-requirements had been laid down for each magistracy. The ideal was to be elected at the minimum age or 'in one's year' as the Romans put it, which Caesar consistently achieved. Every appointment was for one year. Sulla introduced further stipulations to curb the power of ambitious holders of public office.

The lowest rung of the ladder was that of *quaestor*, which an aspiring politician could hold at the age of thirty. Quaestors were in charge of the public treasury and assisted governors in the running of their provinces. Since Sulla's day twenty were elected. In his mid-thirties the career politician could hold the office of an aedileship. There were two *curule* (i.e. patrician) *aediles* and two *plebeian aediles*[4]. Together they supervised certain games, handled the distribution of corn, maintained public order, controlled the public baths and brothels, and ensured minimal standards of public sanitation.

An optional step in the ladder, which none the less conferred prestige upon the incumbent, was that of tribune of the *plebs*. Originally the ten tribunes represented the interests of the common people against the arbitrary exercise of power by patricians, especially those who were magistrates. By the first century BCE, however, most of the ruling élite were plebeians with the result that tribunes frequently found themselves embroiled with other plebeians. The tribunes had extensive powers, including the right to enforce decrees of the *plebs*, and the right to veto senatorial decrees. Sulla excluded tribunes from holding other magistracies, thereby in effect making the tribunate a dead-end job, but in 75 his law was rescinded. Caesar regularly relied upon the services of friendly tribunes to restrain his enemies in the senate during his eight years in Gaul. In fact his ally P. Clodius Pulcher was adopted into a plebeian family so that he could hold the tribunate and use its powers on Caesar's behalf.

At thirty-nine a politician was eligible to be *praetor*. Praetors, eight of whom were elected in Sulla's day, were in charge of both criminal and civil jurisdiction. Finally at forty-two, if he had survived the rough and tumble of politics thus far and if he had enough money to bribe his supporters, he could be *consul*. Strictly speaking, '*nobilis*' was reserved for members of families which had previously held the consulship, though the term was sometimes used more loosely. As we have already seen, *nobilitas* was not a necessary qualification for this office. The two consuls acted as heads of state and supreme military commanders. Each had the power to veto the other's proposals and both were subject to veto by any of the ten tribunes. Elected in July, they took office the following 1st January. Ten years had to elapse before an ex-consul could stand for a second consulship. However, the rules of the *cursus honorum* were frequently being broken by Caesar's day. The most conspicuous offender was Pompey, who at the age of thirty-five was elected consul without having held any lower magistracy.

Finally, in times of emergency, a *dictator* was elected for a period of six months. The Romans always looked fondly back to the ideal incumbent, a farmer named Cincinnatus, who assumed office when Rome was facing attack from a neighbouring tribe called the Aequi. Within the space of fifteen days Cincinnatus had raised an army, defeated the Aequi, celebrated a triumph and resigned from office. Then, during the Punic Wars, Q. Fabius Maximus had held a dictatorship for six months to oppose the invading forces of Hannibal. The institution had remained effectively defunct for 120 years until Sulla, breaking all precedents, was elected dictator 'for the purpose of enacting laws and restoring the Republic'. Caesar held the dictatorship repeatedly from 49 to 44 – initially, like Sulla, 'for the purpose of restoring the Republic' – first for eleven days, then for a year, later for ten years and finally, a month before his death, for life.

There were also deep-seated problems in the way that the empire was governed. Following their year of office in Rome, ex-consuls and ex-praetors were assigned the administration of a province as *proconsul* or *propraetor*. This practice, which was intended to create a balance between political and military office, had the additional benefit of removing ambitious individuals temporarily from Rome. Since magistrates had to invest huge sums of money to run for office and since they did not receive any pay for their services beyond a modest allowance for expenses, many of them looked forward to a lucrative governorship during which they could recoup the exorbitant cost of running a political campaign. The opportunities for mismanagement and extortion by unprincipled governors were enormous. One of the worst offenders was C. Verres, who allegedly extorted 40 million sesterces from Sicily during his two years as its propraetor from 73-71.

Governors who were sent to unpacified provinces sought to cover themselves in *gloria* (military distinction). The attainment of *gloria* was publicly acknowledged by the award of a triumph. To qualify, a governor needed to have presided over the slaughter of at least 5000 of the enemy. No-one achieved more *gloria* than Caesar, which is merely another way of saying that no-one was responsible for more slaughter. At the beginning of Caesar's career, Rome's empire extended from the Straits of Gibraltar to the Euphrates. It included Spain, southern France, Sicily, Corsica and Sardinia, the coastline of Yugoslavia, Macedonia, Greece, western Turkey and Tunisia (fig. 3). Whether Rome acquired her empire deliberately or through a policy of self-defence is a complex question that cannot be addressed here. Yet despite all the political turmoil which Rome underwent during the period of civil war, her grasp upon the empire remained unchallenged.

Governorships were supposed to last a year, but, because of the size and complexity of the empire, they were increasingly being extended or 'prorogued'. Pompey, for instance, was given command of Rome's navy for three years to clear the Mediterranean of pirates at a time when they were threatening Italy with famine, though in the event he managed to complete the job within three months. The following year he received the Asiatic provinces of Cilicia, Bithynia and Pontus (the Black Sea region), in order to conduct war against king Mithridates VI of Pontus, who in 88 had organised the cold-blooded massacre of 80,000 Italian inhabitants of the province of Asia. Pompey's commands paved the way, in terms of duration, for Caesar's proconsulship of Gaul, which lasted nine years. Prorogation tended to intensify the allegiance that soldiers felt towards their general.

This problem was compounded by the fact that from the late first century onwards the majority of legionaries were being recruited from the ranks of the dispossessed poor. On completion of their military service, they therefore looked to their commander for land to settle. Land alone would guarantee them lifelong security, since the concept of a pension did not exist in the ancient world. Had there been no other crisis than this in the late Republic, the allegiance that legions owed to their commanders and the need of those commanders to provide their veterans with land, would have been sufficient to undermine republican institutions. In 88 Sulla's command against Mithridates was transferred to C. Marius, Caesar's uncle by marriage. Marius, who had held six consecutive consulships in the closing years of the second century, was a distinguished general who had won victories both in north Africa and against invading German tribes. Loath to be deprived of the profits of war, Sulla appealed to his legions to march on Rome. They willingly obliged, having nothing to lose and everything to gain, though only one of his officers accompanied them. Again, in 49, at the end of his Gallic command, Caesar took the same action, thereby initiating the Civil War.

From the beginning so far as we know the Roman electoral system employed various intricate systems of group-voting to give precedence to wealth and birth, unlike, say, the Athenian democracy, which was based on the strict principle of one man one vote. There were four different types of Roman assemblies, all of which were summoned mainly to elect magistrates and to ratify or reject bills. The *comitia centuriata* (centuriate assembly or assembly by centuries) elected consuls and praetors, and voted on matters to do with war and peace. The franchise was divided into 197 centuries, according to property qualification. However, there were very many more centuries for the wealthy than there were for the poor. Those in the top property class accounted for 70 centuries; those in the bottom class – the vast majority of the population – for just one. Since the wealthy voted first, moreover, the votes of the lower classes were frequently disregarded. There was similar discrimination in the case of the *comitia tributa* (tribal assembly), which allocated only four of the 35 tribes into which it divided the citizenry to the urban plebs. Compounding the unrepresentative nature of the system was the fact that, although the franchise included all Italy, the rural population, being tied to the land, was unable to vote. It is estimated that of the one million Romans who were entitled to vote in the late Republic only about 10,000 did so on a regular basis. In addition, many of the issues that drive politics today were hardly discussed and never put to a popular vote. Taxation was not a political issue because only the long-suffering inhabitants of the provinces were taxed, which meant in turn that there was never any debate about the economy. Many social problems, such as law enforcement, housing shortage and education were also completely ignored.

We do not know if Roman religion was in crisis in Caesar's day; for we know so little about the belief-system of the man and woman in the street. What is undeniable, however, is that religious office conferred both prestige and patronage. That is why Caesar sought the position. of *pontifex maximus*, the responsibilities of which included general oversight of state cult. Whether Caesar exploited the position for his own ends is impossible to judge, but he certainly saw it as a stepping-stone to higher office.

Since no important decision could be reached without divine approval, 'auspices' had to be taken to determine whether the outcome would be favourable before a meeting of the senate or an assembly could be held. The same practice applied to private households as it did to affairs of state. Taking the auspices meant interpreting the flight or songs of birds, observing the feeding habits of the sacred chickens, or searching the sky for meteorological signs like thunder and lightning. The system allowed for some abuse. During his consulship M. Bibulus sought to prevent his colleague Caesar from passing legislation by repeatedly announcing that he was 'watching the skies' for a sign that would justify the suspension of senatorial business. As Caesar ignored him, his enemies later claimed that his legislation was invalid, though Bibulus' own action may have lacked a constitutional basis.

Resort to violence as a way of resolving conflict was becoming ever more frequent in the late Republic. This was largely the result of a deeply ingrained culture of political corruption, which was now spinning out of control. The first instance of civic violence had occurred in 133 when Ti. Gracchus was clubbed to death by a group of senators anxious to prevent his re-election to the tribunate. The precedent was followed repeatedly over the next hundred years. In addition, bands of thugs increasingly terrorised their opponents, like those of P. Clodius Pulcher and T. Annius Milo (see p. 41). During his consulship, Caesar frequently resorted to violence in order to secure the passage of his legislation.

Lawlessness seethed below the surface of social, as well as political life. A full explanation for the social unrest of the late Republic would require an in-depth sociological analysis of data that we simply do not possess. However, we can identify some of the contributing factors, including indebtedness at all levels of society, overcrowding, urban decay, food shortage, and a growth in the number of private bodyguards. In 63 L. Sergius Catilina (Catiline) stood for the consulship with an ambitious proposal to cancel debts. According to Cicero, whose testimony is partial, he intended to cause an uprising throughout Italy and march on Rome. Largely due to Cicero's efforts, however, Catiline was thwarted (see p. 29 f.).

Rome was heavily overpopulated. Most of the citizenry lived just above the poverty line in conditions that were uncomfortable, unsanitary and hazardous. Effluent flowed through the streets in open drains. The stench was so overpowering that the wealthy held roses to their noses. One imagines that even halitosis, from which the majority of the population suffered, would have presented more than just a minor inconvenience. There were no hospitals, no mental institutions, no old people's homes, and only one, very small prison. Most citizens owned at least one slave, many owned dozens. The streets were filled with beggars, thieves and prostitutes. Though violent crime was commonplace, there was no police force, which meant that those who could afford to do so protected themselves with gangs of vigilantes. Despite the fact that tenement blocks, many of which were five or six stories high, were regularly burning down or imploding under their own weight, often with heavy loss of life, there was only a very rudimentary fire service.

The level of noise would have been intolerable to the modern ear. There was so much traffic that it was eventually decided that wheeled vehicles could only move about at night. Plague and other forms of disease were an annual occurrence. Malnutrition was widespread. Infant mortality was probably as high as 25%. Disability, particularly broken · bones that had never been properly set, affected a large percentage of the population. The average age at death was 34 for women, 46 for men. The economic gap between the poor and wealthy was as extreme as it has been in any society. In sum, it is impossible to estimate the human cost that went into the making of this, the capital of the ancient world.

Chapter 4

The Ambitious Upstart

The Julian *gens* or clan to which C. Julius Caesar belonged was of unparalleled ancestry, claiming descent from Aeneas, founder of the Roman race, and the goddess Venus. It also claimed descent from Proculus Julius, to whom Romulus, the first king of Rome, revealed himself as a god. The origin of the *cognomen*[5] 'Caesar' is unknown. One ancient theory derived it from the word for bluish-grey eyes, another from the African word for elephant.

Even so, Caesar did not begin his career with many advantages. Although the Julii belonged to that privileged group of aristocrats known as patricians, the Caesarian branch of his *gens* was not prominent politically. Only two of his ancestors had held the consulship during the preceding two hundred years. Throughout his career he relied heavily on the support of the common people, who, despite the unrepresentative nature of the republican constitution (see p. 19), could nonetheless voice their will both in public demonstrations of support and through the offices of the tribunes of the *plebs*. He therefore aligned himself with the *populares* (supporters of the common people), as opposed to the *optimates* (the 'best people'), who defended the interests of the élite. In fact Caesar was extremely adept at exploiting the popular will to fulfil his ambition, a circumstance which made him an object of suspicion from the start (Plutarch *JC* 5, 8.3), though we should not assume that he did so entirely cynically. In particular, he supported debt relief for impoverished creditors and the distribution of land to poor citizens, subsidised hand-outs of corn for the population of Rome, and, last but not least, waged profitable wars that increased Rome's wealth.

Caesar's father, also named C. Julius Caesar, only attained the rank of praetor and propraetor. He died of a stroke when Caesar was fifteen, which was the age when a Roman youth first put on the plain white *toga virilis* (toga of manhood), the formal attire of a Roman citizen. (Boys and curule magistrates – magistrates, that is, of patrician stock – wore a *toga praetexta* or toga with a purple border.) Caesar therefore grew up in a household that was dominated by women – his mother Aurelia, his aunt Julia, and his two sisters, both of whom also took the *gens* name Julia (*major* and *minor*), as was traditional practice[6]. It is interesting to speculate how his environment might have formed his character and influenced his outlook, especially in light of the fact that his father's death meant that he became at just fifteen *paterfamilias* (head of the family). This position gave him legal authority over his female relatives – including even his mother – all of whom would have required his consent before marrying.

Caesar's most celebrated relative was C. Marius, the husband of his father's sister, who, as we saw, had held the consulship six times. Partly because his family was in eclipse politically and partly because it was on the losing side in the Civil War waged by Sulla, his career was slow to get underway. He was, therefore, an outsider – a fact which provides an important key to understanding the course and tenor of his public life.

Virtually nothing is known about Caesar's childhood and adolescence. In general, ancient biographers were not interested in their subject's early years, since they did not subscribe to the modern theory that formative experiences condition personality development. Like all young aristocrats Caesar would have had a private tutor (or tutors). Given his accomplishments, he must have been very well-educated. Suetonius (*DJ* 56.7) credits him with a number of youthful compositions, including a work entitled *The Tragedy of Oedipus*, which was probably an abridged translation of Sophocles' celebrated play *Oedipus the King*. He may have been something of a child prodigy, though the concept as such was unknown to the ancient world. Judging from the fact that Caesar chose the occasion of his aunt's funeral to revive the custom of delivering a eulogy on behalf of the deceased, we may conclude that she played a leading role in his upbringing (see p. 26). His sister Julia minor gave birth to a daughter named Atia, who married a certain C. Octavius, a man of modest political ability. She bore him a son of the same name, who, after adoption by Caesar, eventually became the emperor Augustus.

A year after his father's death Caesar broke off his engagement to Cossutia, a girl of undistinguished background, and married Cornelia, the daughter of a prominent patrician called L. Cornelius Cinna. Cinna secured Caesar's appointment as *flamen Dialis* (priest of Jupiter). For some obscure reason this office precluded his advance to the consulship, a fact which interestingly reveals that neither Cinna nor his son-in-law believed at this point that such high aspirations were attainable. The marriage greatly angered Sulla since Cinna belonged to the opposing faction. He annulled the priesthood and demanded that Caesar divorce his wife. Caesar now showed his true colours and flatly refused to obey.

He went into hiding, fearing for his life. Sulla, however, spared him apparently out of respect for his patrician background. Caesar persuaded his mother's cousins to intercede on his behalf and was posted to the staff of the propraetor of Bithynia. During his tour of duty he won the *corona civica* ('civic crown'), the Roman equivalent of the Victoria cross, for repelling an attack by Mithridates, king of Pontus.

While he was out in the east Caesar had a notorious sexual liaison with Nicomedes, king of Bithynia – or so the rumour went. No details survive but, given Nicomedes' Greek background, it may have been the kind of homosexual relationship between an older and a younger man, entered into partly for educational purposes, which Plato describes in his dialogue *The Symposium*. The charge stuck with him till his dying day. When he celebrated his quadruple triumph thirty-five years later (p. 54), he was mocked by his soldiers for being Nicomedes' catamite. Such mockery, incidentally, was in accordance with the traditional Roman practice of seeking to avert the anger of the gods from any exceptionally successful individual by drawing attention to their flaws or faults. Caesar, however, was enraged. A few days later he took a solemn oath denying the charge in the presence of Rome's religious establishment, hoping to scotch it once and for all, but only succeeded in making himself look more ridiculous. Though not homophobic *per se*, the Romans held to the opinion that only slaves and degenerates would submit to buggery. The allegation belonged to the traditional Greek and Roman image of the tyrant as a depraved sexual pervert. It was therefore not only humiliating but also politically damaging. (In later times allegations of sexual depravity became part of the stereotypical image of 'bad' Roman emperors, such as we find in Suetonius' characterisation of both Tiberius and Caligula.)

Learning of Sulla's death Caesar returned to Rome in 79. He was just 21. He now took the conventional first steps of a career in politics by seeking to build up his reputation as an orator. Since there was no public prosecutor in Rome, provincials with complaints against Roman officials had to rely on the services of an inexperienced but up-and-coming orator. Caesar's early legal career was typical of many ambitious young men. He brought an unsuccessful charge against Cn. Cornelius Dolabella, a supporter of Sulla, for extorting money from the province of Macedonia. The following year he prosecuted C. Antonius, one of Sulla's ex-officers, for enriching himself in the war against Mithridates. Again he was unsuccessful; but he had at least drawn attention to himself. He decided to go to Rhodes to hone his oratorical skills under a Greek orator. Although it became regular practice in imperial times for aristocratic Romans to complete their education in Greece, this was not yet the case. The decision is therefore evidence of his personal regard for Greek culture.

On his way to Rhodes, Caesar was captured and ransomed by pirates. Once freed, he secured a fleet and captured his captors. He then went to the governor of Asia and asked that the pirates be brought to justice. While the governor dallied, hoping to make a profit out of the incident, Caesar took matters into his own hands and had the pirates crucified. The story goes that he played games with his captors and recited poetry to them, chiding them for their lack of education. When he learnt that they had set his ransom at a 'mere' 48,000 sesterces he insisted that they raise it to 1,200,000 sesterces. Finally, Caesar threatened to crucify them if they ever released him – a threat he duly carried out. The anecdote speaks volumes about certain traits in Caesar's character, as it is surely meant to do – his intellectual sophistication, his dauntless demeanour, his disdain for death, and his intense preoccupation with his own *dignitas*. Since the only surviving witness for his sojourn with the pirates was Caesar himself, however, it is more than likely that the claims are of his own invention and that he circulated them to promote his public image.

Caesar remained in the east for two or three years, successfully fending off Mithridates' attempt to destabilise the province of Asia. Then, on learning that he had been co-opted to the college of pontiffs, he returned to Rome. In 71 he was elected military tribune, one of the six senior officers assigned to each legion. He spoke in favour of an amnesty for the supporters of M. Aemilius Lepidus who had enriched themselves during the Sullan proscriptions. It was the same year that M. Licinius Crassus finally managed to suppress the famous slave revolt in Capua led by the Thracian gladiator Spartacus, who raised a force of 70,000 and defeated two consular armies. Two years later, aged thirty, Caesar became quaestor and was posted to the province of Further (i.e. south-east) Spain.

Before he departed his aunt Julia and his wife Cornelia both died. These losses must have come as a bitter blow. His aunt was in all probability the most important influence in his life following the death of his father; Cornelia had borne him Julia, his only certain offspring. He delivered his aunt's funerary oration in the forum, proclaiming the fact that the Julian *gens* was descended both from Venus and from Ancus Martius, Rome's second king. We do not know whether Caesar had any belief in such claims, though they undoubtedly enhanced his profile. As an act of deliberate bravado, calculated to offend the supporters of Sulla, he displayed the *imago* (wax image) of his uncle Marius in her funeral procession. He may also have displayed Cinna's *imago* at Cornelia's funeral.

His biographers report that, while he was in Spain, Caesar saw a statue of Alexander the Great in the temple of Hercules at Cadiz. The sight made him groan aloud at the poverty of his own achievement compared with that of his predecessor who, at his age, had already conquered the whole known world. The anecdote suggests that he had already made up his mind at this early point in his career to be spectacular. Though Caesar may have disseminated the story to invite comparison between himself and the greatest military genius that the Greek world ever produced, it is also possible that it was invented by Plutarch to justify his pairing of Alexander with Caesar (see p. 10).

On his return from Spain, Caesar married Sulla's grand-daughter Pompeia (no relation to Pompey), though he did not use the occasion to make any overtures to the Sullan party. He supported the two laws conferring extraordinary commands on Pompey, whom he now came to regard as a useful patron. Then in 65 he became *curule aedile*. His enemies traced his desire to establish a *regnum* or despotism to the early days of his aedileship, taking as their cue the fact that he now began to display an aptitude for self-promotion and the manipulation of public opinion. Suetonius (*DJ* 9.2), drawing on a variety of hostile sources, alleges that shortly before taking office he entered into a conspiracy to give Crassus the dictatorship. Plutarch (*JC* 6) claims that he used his office to restore the reputation of his uncle Marius and advance the cause of his party. He did this by ordering that the images of Marius and of the goddess Victory be set up on the Capitol. As a result, some senators protested that Caesar was seeking to establish a tyranny. While Suetonius' allegation is almost certainly the product of malicious gossip, Plutarch's claim is entirely plausible. Though his aedileship may have been the pivotal moment that first brought Caesar into an awareness of his own extraordinary talents, we should not assume that he had mapped out the future course of his career in any detail.

Caesar was the first politician to comprehend that gladiatorial contests could be used to gain popularity. Until now such contests were permitted only at funerals, the belief being that the souls of the departed could best be appeased by the shedding of human blood (fig. 4). In early times the Romans merely offered sacrificial victims at the graveside. These would usually be either prisoners of war or condemned criminals. Only later did they require the victims to fight to the death. Caesar now bent the rules by sponsoring a contest in memory of his father, who had died twenty years previously. Determined to put on the most lavish display that Rome had ever witnessed, he purchased 320 pairs of gladiators whom he decked out in silver armour. The games were held in the Roman forum, the customary venue at this time for such entertainments. The show instantly made the donor recognisable to the entire urban *plebs*, whose support he could count on when he next stood for public office. Incidentally, his colleague as curule aedile was M. Calpurnius Bibulus. It was the kind of unfortunate match that the republican system tended to produce from time to time, since the two men, who had a visceral dislike for one

Fig. 4 Gladiatorial combat at a Roman funeral

another, were destined to become colleagues again both as praetors and as consuls.

Caesar did not have to wait long to capitalise on his popularity. The following year the life-time position of *pontifex maximus* fell vacant. In addition to supervising state cult, the pontifex maximus regulated the calendar, which Caesar took it upon himself to reform, since the official (lunar) calendar consistently lagged behind the solar year. Though the office was usually filled by an ex-consul, Caesar saw it as a way of catapulting himself to prominence, and he boldly announced his candidacy. He proceeded to court the *plebs* and resorted to bribery on a massive scale. 'Either I shall return as *pontifex maximus* or not at all', he told his mother on the morning of the election (Plutarch *JC* 7). He knew that he was a marked man and that he had made dangerous enemies.

After winning the election, Caesar moved from his modest dwelling in a run-down district known as the Subura and took up residence in the *domus publica* (state house) in the centre of the Roman Forum (fig. 5). It was one of the most prestigious addresses in Rome. Apart from the Vestal virgins, who tended Rome's sacred hearth, the *pontifex maximus* and his household were the only residents. The *domus publica* was part of a cluster of religious buildings that included the temple of Vesta and the *regia* (or palace), which contained the offices of the *pontifex maximus* and his staff.

The forum was the political, civic and religious heart of the city. It was also its commercial and legal centre. The location was thus commensurate with the increasing control that Caesar would now begin to exercise over these varied aspects of Roman life. Roughly rectangular in shape, the forum measured about 200 metres in length by 75 metres in breadth. Some distance from the *domus publica* were situated the *curia* (senate house) and the circular *comitium* (assembly ground). The long sides of the forum were lined with basilicas or colonnaded halls, containing shops, offices and meeting places. The space was traversed by a flag-stoned road known as the *via sacra* (sacred way), lined throughout its length with statues and notice boards.

We now come to a very obscure incident in his life. Caesar, along with Crassus, had supported the revolutionary L. Sergius Catilina (Catiline) in his unsuccessful bid for the consulship of 63. Catiline stood again for office the following year with a proposal to cancel all debts, only to be defeated a second time, largely due to the scare-mongering tactics employed by Cicero who was now consul. Catiline, therefore, conspired to overthrow the Republic – or at least that is what Cicero alleged. Caesar, who was charged with involvement in his treasonable schemes, quickly moved to distance himself from Catiline. He nonetheless spoke against the summary execution of his five fellow-supporters, on the grounds that this would set a dangerous legal precedent. Instead he recommended that they be imprisoned in various towns outside Rome.

We should note that the Roman penal system very rarely passed the death penalty on its citizens. Much more common were loss of civic rights, confiscation of property and exile. Prisons were used only as places of temporary confinement. Caesar's proposal of imprisonment thus reflected recognition of the gravity of the situation.

However, M. Porcius Cato, a self-righteous firebrand who made a virtue of austerity, spoke vehemently against the proposal, claiming that Caesar was implicated in the conspiracy. Plutarch tells us that Cato challenged Caesar to read a letter that was delivered to him during a meeting of the senate, in the belief that it had been written by Catiline – only to discover that it was a love-letter written to Caesar by his half-sister Servilia. Undaunted, Cato managed to secure the rejection of

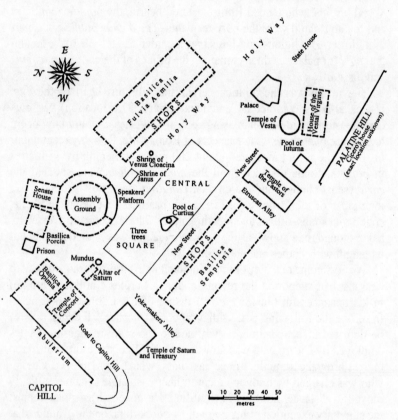

Fig. 5 The Roman Forum, plan

Caesar's proposal; and the five men were summarily executed without a proper trial. The degree to which Caesar was involved remains unclear but the conspiracy afforded useful ammunition to his enemies, who were becoming increasingly suspicious and resentful of his prominence.

The following year Caesar held the praetorship, during which he campaigned vigorously for the recall of Pompey to help quell Catiline's forces. His action antagonised those members of the senate who were seeking to postpone the land grant to Pompey's veterans and the ratification of his eastern settlement. Pompey had conquered much of the Near East, including Syria and Judaea (modern Israel and Palestine), reducing the latter to the status of a client kingdom.

Then in December Caesar's private life was seriously disrupted. A certain quaestor-designate named P. Clodius Pulcher succeeded in gaining entry to his house, where nocturnal rites in honour of the *bona dea* (good goddess) were being celebrated in the presence of the Vestal virgins. It was alleged that Clodius was seeking to further an adulterous relationship with Pompeia, though a religious festival hardly provided the most suitable occasion for conducting a clandestine affair. Since men were debarred from witnessing these rites, which were supervised by the wife of a consul or praetor, he had sought to gain entry by disguising himself as a woman. Clodius was apprehended by a slave girl and exposed. Later he was brought to trial before a tribunal set up by the senate on the charge of sacrilege. Caesar, however, refused to testify against him and Clodius was acquitted. The most plausible explanation behind Caesar's action is that he did not wish to deprive himself of Clodius' political support. He nonetheless divorced Pompeia, declaring that 'Caesar's wife must be above suspicion' (Plutarch *JC* 10). He could hardly have made a more overt declaration of the importance that he placed on his public image. At the same time, the incident provided him with the excuse to form a more politically advantageous marital alliance.

In 61 Caesar was appointed *propraetor* of Further Spain. Like most aspiring politicians, he was by now heavily in debt and had to borrow a vast sum of money from M. Licinius Crassus to prevent his creditors from debarring him from leaving the capital. Crassus, a former supporter of Sulla, had made his fortune by purchasing the properties of the 'proscribed' at knockdown prices. During his time in Spain, Caesar conquered Lusitania (roughly corresponding to modern Portugal) and was awarded a triumph. He now coveted the consulship; but the law required that he lay down his command before announcing his candidacy. Though most of the senate was prepared to grant him a special dispensation, Cato vigorously protested. Once again his objections carried the day. Caesar decided to give priority to his political aspirations. Accordingly he renounced his military command, thus foregoing the triumph, and returned to Rome as a private citizen.

Caesar now took the bold and imaginative step of concluding a secret deal with Crassus and Pompey, the two most powerful men of their day. Though previously antagonistic to one another, they had both been thwarted by the senate, which had refused to pass legislation in their favour. Pompey, as we have seen, was eager that the political settlement he had made in the east should be ratified and his veterans given land. Crassus wanted the tax collectors of Asia to be granted remission for one-third of the sum that they owed to the government.[7]

Caesar undertook to force all these measures through if elected consul. In turn Pompey and Crassus agreed to support him by bribery and influence. As a reward he was to receive after his consulship a plum province, which he needed to clear his huge debts. The senate, anticipating Caesar's election, sought to thwart him, by announcing in advance of the elections that the successful candidates would be assigned the superintendence of the forests and cattle-tracks of Italy as their 'provinces'.

The agreement that Caesar forged with Pompey and Crassus is sometimes inaccurately termed the 'first triumvirate' to distinguish it from the very different arrangement made between Octavian, Mark Antony and M. Lepidus after Caesar's assassination. Apart from the fact that Caesar was its instigator, we know nothing about its internal workings. What held it together, however, was Caesar's political skills, which neutralised the antipathy between his two partners. Unlike the 'second triumvirate', it was an informal *amicitia* (political alliance) with no constitutional basis whatsoever. Syme (1939, 35 f.) described it as 'a capture of the constitution', since the three men now proceeded to secure the election of their supporters; and it led, ultimately, to civil war. It was appropriate, therefore, that C. Asinius Pollio chose to begin his history of the Civil War in the year 60. In essence, however, the first triumvirate was merely an agreement to pool political resources, and it cannot in itself be considered illegal.

Caesar took office as consul on 1st January 59. His colleague was Cato's son-in-law Bibulus (with whom he had also served his aedileship and praetorship). He, like Caesar, had secured his election by massive bribery. Caesar, intent on passing an ambitious raft of measures and faced with intransigence, resorted to blatant intimidation. Bibulus, who on one occasion had a bucket of manure emptied over his head (Plutarch, *Pompey* 48.1), retired to his home and, as previously noted, declared that he was 'watching the skies' and that all senatorial business had to be suspended. Wags observed that they were living under the consulship of Julius and Caesar, as Caesar now did the work of two men. Frustrated by the senate he went directly to the people and, with the support of P. Vatinius, tribune of the *plebs*, had his proposals passed. At no point in his career prior to his crossing of the Rubicon did Caesar come closer to breaking the law. Though the senate could have voted to invalidate his legislation, either by endorsing Bibulus' objections or by accusing him of resorting to force, for whatever motive it refrained from doing so.

Caesar's most important piece of legislation was a bill to distribute state-owned land in Campania to the poor.[8] This was the agriculturally prosperous region outside Rome. The measure was highly unpopular with members of the aristocracy, who had been leasing the land. High on his agenda, too, was a bill to give land to Pompey's veterans. In addition, Caesar passed a law against extortion by Roman officials in the provinces, drew up a detailed charter regulating provincial administration and ratified Pompey's eastern settlement. He also published the proceedings of the senate and the popular assemblies in a daily bulletin – the forerunner of the tabloid newspaper, so to speak.

Before the end of the year Caesar, Pompey and Crassus had decided to extend their agreement in order to safeguard their own interests. To strengthen the bond, Caesar offered his daughter Julia to Pompey in marriage. He himself married Calpurnia, the daughter of L. Calpurnius Piso, consul-elect for 58. The tribune P. Vatinius proposed that he receive a five-year special command over the provinces of Illyricum (the coastal strip of Dalmatia extending from the Adriatic to the Danube) and Cisalpine Gaul (Gaul this-side-of-the-Alps, now northern Italy). The precedent for such a governorship had been set by the special commands awarded to Pompey in 67 and 66, the first for the purpose of ridding the Mediterranean of pirates, and the second for the purpose of defeating Mithridates of Pontus (p. 18). Cowed into submission the senate obligingly added Transalpine Gaul.

Before he left for his province, moderates attempted reconciliation by offering to re-enact Caesar's legislation with all due legal process. Caesar rejected their proposal which he regarded as a slight to his *dignitas*. His relationship with the senate had been damaged irreparably. Early in 58 he headed north to take up his commission. What prompted him to go west and intervene in Gaul, rather than turn east and initiate a campaign in Illyricum, where a tribe known as the Getae were threatening to spill into northeast Italy, is a complete mystery.

Chapter 5

The Proconsul of Gaul

Rome's first contact with the Gauls, dates from *ca* 400 when a large contingent left their homeland in the Danube region and swept westwards in migration. Under a chieftain named Brennus they invaded Italy in *ca* 387 and sacked Rome, after inflicting a heavy defeat on her legions. According to the historian Livy (5.48.9), it was one of the darkest chapters in Rome's history and a colourful story is told of how her sacred geese saved the Capitol while the guards slept. When the Romans sought to buy Brennus off and objected that he had tampered with the scales which had been set up to weigh the ransom that had to be paid in gold, Brennus placed his sword in one of the pans and said, 'woe to the conquered!'

The Romans never forgot their humiliation. Even in Caesar's day, they continued to regard the Gauls with pathological fear, a circumstance that Caesar exploited to his advantage. Following his assassination, there was concern that the Gauls would overrun Italy (Cicero, *Letters to Friends* 14.1). We should not minimize the degree of paranoia: for it also helps to explain how it came about that Caesar was given a free rein as proconsul. At the same time the Romans despised the Gauls for their alleged cultural inferiority, a belief which Caesar himself seems to have shared. In fact he does not bother to provide his readers with a description of their culture until the sixth year of his campaign, and even then his remarks are somewhat superficial and borrowed in part from earlier ethnographies (*GW* 6.11-28).

Gaul was by no means a complete backwater. In the central area the inhabitants lived in prosperous urban communities, though their political system was essentially tribal. They were famed for their metalwork. Their pottery was of a very high quality. They grew corn on a large scale. Gold and silver coinage was in circulation. There was a limited degree of literacy. In Caesar's day their population is put at ten million very approximately.

The geopolitical entity called Gaul was very largely a construct of the Roman imagination (fig. 6). Though its population was predominantly

Celtic, Germanic tribes occupied the north-east; Ligurians and Iberians the south. The chief language was Gaulish. The tribes of Britain, who spoke a variant called British, were also Celtic. Before Caesar's conquest, Gaul was divided into two sections called Cisalpine and Transalpine Gaul ('this-side-of-the Alps' and 'across-the-Alps' respectively). Cisalpine Gaul, which had long been pacified, included the region of northern Italy that extends from the Apennines to the Alps. Transalpine Gaul included the area from the Pyrenees in the south to the English channel in the north, and from the Atlantic Ocean in the west to the Rhine in the east. As Caesar famously states in the opening sentence of his *Commentary on the Gallic Wars,* Transalpine Gaul was divided into three parts according to tribal affiliation, Belgae, Aquitani and Galli. The southern part of Transalpine Gaul, known today as Provence (from the Latin word *provincia,* 'province'), had been subjugated in 128 in order to protect the trade route between Italy and Spain. The northern part was referred to disparagingly as *Gallia comata* or long-haired Gaul. The pejorative designation tells us much about the Roman preference for a short-back-and-sides haircut. It was *Gallia comata* which Caesar sought to bring under Roman control. It included northern France, southern Holland, Belgium, Germany west of the Rhine, and most of Switzerland.

Caesar achieved his military objective thanks to the courage, discipline and efficiency of his legions, whose effectiveness as a fighting unit has no parallel in ancient or modern warfare. Legionaries were accustomed to long marches, which they accomplished carrying sixty pounds of equipment on their backs, in addition to arms and armour. Their chief weapons were the two-edged sword and the heavy throwing spear. Their discipline and training vastly exceeded anything that the Gauls could throw against them. As Caesar memorably remarked, they could 'storm the heavens' (*Spanish War* 42.7). Throughout the nine years' war in Gaul, they never faltered and they never mutinied.

A legion comprised between four and six thousand men, sub-divided into ten cohorts, the chief tactical units. The ensign of a legion was an eagle mounted on a pole and each cohort had a *signum* or standard. The nominal commanders of a legion were the six military tribunes. Since many tribunes were young men with little experience of war, Caesar tended to rely instead on his *legati* (legates), usually men of senatorial rank, each in charge of a legion. More important in the heat of battle were the centurions, of whom there were six to each cohort. Centurions were promoted from the ranks in recognition of their bravery and leadership. In hand-to-hand fighting their casualty rate was often disproportionate to their numbers, as proved by the fact that, when Caesar suffered his most

Map of Gallia

BRITANNIA

EBURONES

NERVII

REMI

Lutetia

PARISII

Alesia

VENETI

AEDUI

HELVETII

Gergovia

Uxellodunum

ARVERNI

GALLIA CISALPINA

AQUITANI

PROVINCIA

R. Rhenus

R. Rhodanus

Pyrenees

```
0  25  50      100
▬▬▬▬▬▬▬▬▬▬▬ Miles

0    50  100     200
▬▬▬▬▬▬▬▬▬▬▬ Kilometers
```

– ▪ – ▪ – Boundary of province where known

Fig. 6

serious defeat in the war, he lost as many as 46 centurions compared with fewer than 700 legionaries (*GW* 7.51).

At the outset of his proconsulship Caesar had four legions under his command. In the course of his campaign he enlisted first four, then later two more, so that he ultimately had a force of about 50,000. He was able to increase his fighting strength with comparative ease because Cisalpine and Transalpine Gaul were major recruiting grounds. Caesar also relied upon an unknown number of light-armed troops, primarily Numidians (a north African tribe), Cretans and Balearics.

By contrast the Gallic forces were ill-disciplined and disorganised. We have no accurate knowledge of their numbers – Caesar's figures are undoubtedly inflated – but we can be certain that they enjoyed a considerable numerical advantage. Had they united they would easily have seen off the threat of conquest, but they were perpetually distracted by local jealousies and weakened by petty conflicts. The problem was very largely one of perception. The inhabitants of the territory that the Romans designated Gaul did not primarily regard themselves as Celts, still less as Gauls. In spite of their common culture, they had no tradition of political unity. Rather they thought of themselves exclusively in terms of tribal affiliation. For this reason they never produced a concerted strategy except when they finally rose in revolt, by which time it was too late. Only the Helvetii and the Nervii were up to the challenge of meeting the Romans in pitched battle. Only one Gallic chieftain, Vercingetorix, displayed a true sense of leadership.

It is not clear what instructions the senate gave Caesar when he took up his commission, though it certainly did not authorise him to conquer free Gaul. He did so because a fortuitous set of events gave him the excuse to make war in the name of what we would call national security. Since we have only his *Commentaries* to go on, much remains obscure. Caesar never suggests that his intention was to conquer the whole of Gaul. Nor, of course, did he inform the long-haired Gauls of his plans. Instead he repeatedly pretended to be representing the interests of one tribe against another.

As was the norm in the ancient world, most of the campaigning took place in the summer months. This enabled Caesar to keep fully abreast of political developments in Rome, since he spent all but three winters in Cisalpine Gaul where he was easily contactable. He also utilised the services of tribunes of the *plebs* to represent his interests in the senate and he corresponded regularly with his agents in the capital, primarily the wealthy equestrian L. Cornelius Balbus and the shadowy C. Oppius. He even devised a secret code for matters that were confidential.

In the spring of 58 the Helvetii[9] requested permission to enter Transalpine Gaul on their way westwards to the Bay of Biscay, where they intended to settle. Though they assured him that they had no hostile intent, Caesar denied their request recalling to mind, as he informs his readers, how back in 107 their ancestors had sent a Roman army under the yoke – an act of ritual humiliation (*GW* 1.7). The Helvetii, probably some 250,000 in all, entered Transalpine Gaul despite Caesar's refusal, thereby providing him with a heaven-sent opportunity to start a major war. He immediately raised three legions, struck north and drove them back into Switzerland. Shortly afterwards he defeated Ariovistus, the king of a German tribe known as the Suebi who were moving across the Rhine.

The following year he raised three more legions and began his conquest in earnest. On his way north, however, he was attacked by the Nervii, inhabitants of modern Belgium. Only as a result of Caesar's exemplary personal courage did his legions eventually secure a victory. The Nervii were heavily defeated. At the end of the year Caesar prematurely announced that Gaul had been pacified. The senate rewarded him with an official *supplicatio* or thanksgiving for a military victory, which lasted fifteen days.

In Rome meanwhile a move was under way to strip Caesar of his command and to prevent him from holding any further public office. A bitter enemy L. Domitius Ahenobarbus, confident of being elected consul, declared he would recall Caesar and prosecute him for the illegalities he had committed during his consulship. Caesar entered into further negotiations with Pompey and Crassus, whom he met at Luca (modern Lucca). In addition to an extension to his governorship, he wanted the senate to recognise his conquest of Gaul. It was agreed that Pompey and Crassus should be elected consuls, the former receiving the provinces of Nearer and Further Spain, the latter that of Syria. On assuming office they would pass a law extending Caesar's term as proconsul by forbidding any discussion of his successor until 1st March 50. Having settled matters, Caesar campaigned against rebellious maritime tribes in Brittany and Normandy. He also waged a successful campaign against the Aquitani, who lived on the French side of the Pyrenees close to the Spanish border.

Caesar began the next campaigning season by conducting operations against the Usipetes and Tencteri, German tribes who had crossed the Rhine close to its estuary. To force them back, he bridged the Rhine – the first time in history such a feat had been accomplished. Later in the year he undertook a reconnaissance mission to Britain with two legions. His ostensible purpose was to prevent the British from rendering assistance to their Gallic counterparts, though the island's reputed mineral wealth no doubt acted as a further incentive. The campaign was not a success. Caesar had made little preparation and knew virtually nothing about the enemy's strength. He had never encountered anything comparable to the British war chariots, which were easily manoeuvrable and extremely fast. In addition, his mediterranean-style ships were ill-adapted to the tidal conditions of the English Channel. Consequently, a number were wrecked by a storm, while drawn up on the beach in shallow waters. After narrowly rescuing one of his legions from disaster, he made a hurried departure across the Channel. Once back in Gaul he claimed a military victory, despite the fact that only two of the tribes who promised to send him hostages fulfilled their obligation. Even so, the senate awarded him a *supplicatio* lasting twenty days – five days more than the one he had received for 'pacifying' the whole of Gaul. Britain was thought to lie at the outermost limits of the world and Caesar earned credit principally, we may suspect, for having successfully undertaken the crossing.

In 54 Caesar returned to Britain. This time he brought five of his eight legions and remained in the island for several months. He does not tell us what he hoped to achieve by his second 'invasion'. Perhaps he merely wanted to restore his injured pride. His engineers had designed a vessel with a shallower draught – the first amphibious landing craft in the history of warfare. After a protracted campaign he crossed the Thames at Brentford and defeated Casivellaunus, a chieftain of unknown tribal affiliation who had effectively made himself leader of the British, at Wheathampstead in Hertfordshire. In September word reached him of an uprising in Gaul and once again he hurriedly returned to the continent.

Caesar's second invasion of Britain, like the first, brought no noticeable gains. More importantly it placed his entire conquest of Gaul in jeopardy. It thus raises serious questions about his grasp of strategy. Though the Britons agreed to pay tribute and provide hostages, they again failed to deliver. Cicero, for one, was dismissive of the undertaking and it may well be that his opinion was shared by the majority. The Romans showed no further interest in the island until the emperor Claudius finally conquered much of it in CE 43.

While Caesar was seeking to regain control of the situation in Gaul, Ambiorix, the leader of a Belgic tribe known as the Eburones, who lived close to the Rhine, massacred one and a half of his legions encamped near Liège. Shortly afterwards the Nervii rose in revolt and were barely checked from destroying a Roman camp by the hasty arrival of Caesar himself. Caesar raised two more legions and borrowed a third from Pompey. Around the same time his beloved daughter Julia died in childbirth. He and Pompey were united in their grief. Though the marriage had been promoted to foster their political alliance, Pompey was a devoted husband.

Caesar spent the following year conducting punitive strikes against rebel tribes. He caught the Nervii unawares and forced them to surrender. Then he turned with lightning speed against the Eburones, calling upon neighbouring tribes still friendly to Rome to 'wipe out their race and name as a punishment for their crime' (*GW* 6.34), evidently because he did not want his own soldiers to commit such an atrocity. Ambiorix himself escaped and was never captured. Shortly afterwards Caesar received news that Crassus' army had been annihilated at Carrhae on the Turkish-Syrian border. The latter's death, following so soon after that of Julia, ruptured Caesar's alliance with Pompey and made an eventual showdown inevitable, even though the two initially tried to maintain the fiction of 'business as usual'.

In Rome meanwhile anarchy increasingly prevailed. It culminated in the killing of P. Clodius Pulcher – the man previously suspected of having an affair with Caesar's wife Pompeia – by T. Annius Milo. A pitched battle took place between their rival bands of thugs just outside Rome on the Appian Way. Widespread rioting broke out at Clodius' funeral, culminating in the burning down of the *curia* (senate house), which served as Clodius' funeral pyre. The senate passed emergency measures and elected Pompey as sole consul. Effectively dictator, he nonetheless avoided the odium of the title. Pompey restored order by treating Rome as a turbulent province. Since the existing courts were incapable of dealing with the crisis, he introduced a bill *de vi* (on violence) in order to bring Milo to justice. Milo was unsuccessfully defended by Cicero, his long-time political ally, and went into exile.

As a gesture of goodwill towards Caesar, Pompey had the tribunes sponsor a law which would permit him to stand for the consulship in his absence, an irregularity not permitted by the constitution. This meant that Caesar would not have to lay down his command and return to Rome as a private citizen – an action that would have again denied him a triumph and exposed him to prosecution by his enemies. As if he had second thoughts, however, Pompey enacted that candidates for the consulship must announce their candidacy in Rome. In addition, he extended the term of his own governorship of Spain for four (or five) years. Even now Caesar attempted to shore up their crumbling *amicitia* by offering to divorce his new bride Calpurnia and marry Pompey's daughter. Pompey. snubbed him by marrying the daughter of his bitter foe, Q. Caecilius Metellus Pius Scipio. Caesar responded by securing the services of the tribune C. Scribonius Curio to veto any attempt to advance discussion of his successor in Gaul.[10]

In 52 much of Gaul rose in revolt. Most of the tribes of central, western and northern Gaul eventually joined in. The leader of the revolt was Vercingetorix, the young charismatic chief of the Arverni, inhabitants of the present-day Auvergne region. Correctly surmising that his opponent could more easily be driven out by famine than by the sword, Vercingetorix sought to block off Caesar's supply route. It was the first time during the war that the Gauls had demonstrated any long-term strategy. Vercingetorix inflicted a crushing defeat on Caesar at Gergovia, the capital of the Arverni, four miles south of modern Clermont-Ferrand. Following news of this disaster even the Aedui, Rome's previously staunch allies, threw in their lot with Vercingetorix.

Caesar responded with his customary enterprise and daring. He hired a force of German cavalry, narrowly escaped an ambush and forced Vercingetorix to withdraw to Alesia (now Alise-Sainte-Reine near Dijon), a natural fortress over 150 metres high. He then proceeded to surround it with eight bases, so as to starve Vercingetorix into submission. He also built a defensive cordon eleven miles long and laid trenches and booby traps consisting of pits filled with deadly wooden spikes and iron objects. Learning that a relief army was on its way, he hurriedly built a second defensive cordon fourteen miles in length facing in the opposite direction. Confronted by enemies on both sides, Caesar repelled their combined forces and won an outstanding victory, ably aided by his German cavalry, who caught the enemy in the rear. He claims he was outnumbered by five to one.

There was still unrest in Gaul the following year. The final engagement took place at another hill fortress called Uxellodunum (perhaps modern Puy d'Issolde), which Caesar captured by diverting its water supply. He then ordered his men to chop off the right hands of all their captives. According to Asinius Pollio, who takes up the narrative at this point, Caesar acted not in the spirit of vengeance but to hasten the end of the revolt (*GW* 8.44). The policy succeeded. He then imposed a fairly lenient settlement, allowing the Gauls to collect their own tribute and leaving their tribal institutions largely intact. Many Gauls who had supported him during the revolt were rewarded with the name 'Julius' (French: Jules).

Caesar conquered Gaul by disguising his true intentions and constantly playing one tribe off against another. He took the unilateral decision to romanise Gaul primarily to enhance his military reputation and increase his power base. He did not concern himself with the welfare of the region, which he shamelessly exploited for his own personal enrichment. Like most of his countrymen, he saw nothing to admire and little worth preserving in Gallic culture.

If Caesar were alive today he would certainly be guilty of crimes against humanity. As Christian Meier (1982, 258) put it, his conquest of Gaul was 'an enormity even by contemporary standards', since the Gauls posed no immediate threat to Rome's security. Some sixty Gallic tribes lost their independence; others were annihilated altogether. On the basis of Caesar's own figures, Plutarch calculates that he killed a million Gauls and enslaved a million others. The fact that Caesar almost certainly exaggerated the number is evidence of the degree to which he considered such loss of human life fully justified. Not the least of the charges that can be laid against him is the fact that he kept Vercingetorix in captivity for six years, merely to parade him in his triumph before having him garrotted immediately afterwards.[11]

Chapter 6

The Gambler

The Civil War might easily have been avoided. All it would have taken is a modicum of commonsense and restraint on the part of the senate. Caesar was justifiably concerned about the precariousness of his position as the year 50 drew to its close. After all, his enemies had made it abundantly clear that they intended to prosecute him as soon as he laid down his command. That at least is how Caesar viewed the impasse.

On 1st December the tribune M. Scribonius Curio put a motion to the senate recommending that both Caesar and Pompey be relieved of their commands. 370 senators voted in favour, only 22 against (Appian *CW* 2.30). Instead of accepting this for what it was – a vote for peace – the consul C. Claudius Marcellus worked the senate into a state of hysteria, by exploiting a rumour that Caesar was already marching on Rome. Accompanied by both consuls designate for 49, Marcellus went to Pompey with a sword which he placed in his hands. He then conferred upon him the command of the two legions that had been assigned to Caesar for a campaign against the Parthians. (The objective of the campaign had been to avenge Crassus' defeat at Carrhae and to retrieve the legionary eagles lost there.) Pompey now undertook the defence of the city against Caesar.

Attempts to negotiate a settlement over the course of the next month were met with intransigence by Pompey. On 1st January the tribunes M. Antonius, better known as Mark Antony (pl. v), and M. Cassius forced the newly elected consul L. Cornelius Lentulus Crus to read a letter from Caesar addressed to the senate. In it he enumerated all his services to the state, pointed out that he had been given the right to stand for the consulship *in absentia*, and proposed either that he be allowed to keep his provinces until after the elections had taken place or that he and Pompey should simultaneously lay down their commissions. He ended by threatening civil war if Pompey failed to comply. Lentulus, however, refused to allow Caesar's proposal to be put to the vote. Instead a motion declaring him to be a public enemy was passed but vetoed in turn by Antony. The senate had effectively reached deadlock. Further negotiations took place over the course of the next few days. On 7th January, at the prompting of Lentulus, the senate passed the *senatus consultum ultimum* ('last decree of the senate'), instructing himself and his colleague to 'see that no harm befall the Republic'. Fearing for their lives, the Caesarian tribunes, accompanied by Curio, left the city in disguise and headed north to join Caesar.

The senate had presented Caesar with two stark options: either he could surrender his legions and submit to certain exile and possible execution; alternatively, he could do what Sulla had done before and march on Rome. The news of the senate's decision reached him at Ravenna, then in Cisalpine Gaul, on 10th January, where he had in his own words, 'been waiting for an answer to his very mild demands in the hope that the people's sense of natural justice would bring the matter to a peaceable conclusion' (*CW* 1.5.3). He acted with characteristic decisiveness – and deceptiveness. He pretended to separate from his troops and spent the evening dining with friends. Then, at the river Rubicon, the dividing line between Cisalpine Gaul and Italy where generals were required by ancient law to lay down their commissions, he rejoined his troops. There he considered his options with his friends, chief of whom according to Plutarch (*JC* 32) was C. Asinius Pollio, the future historian of the Civil War. 'My friends, to leave this stream uncrossed will breed much trouble for me. To cross it – for all mankind', he observed. Suetonius (*DJ* 31) claims that his hesitancy was resolved by an apparition, who seized a trumpet from one of his men and sounded the call to arms. More plausible is the anecdote that he quoted a line from the Greek poet Menander, 'let the die be cast', before crossing the stream at the head of his army.

Caesar marched throughout the night and entered Ariminum (modern Rimini) at dawn (fig. 2). As the inscription in the main square records, he harangued his troops, and probably the local population too, seeking to convince them of the justice of his cause. Then he continued south along the *via Flaminia*.

The Civil War was fought not for the sake of principles but for self-interest. As the poet Lucan (*CW* 1.125 f.) memorably put it, 'Caesar could not tolerate any superior nor Pompey any equal'. At the outset both men tried to clothe their dispute in high-sounding phrases, though they can have deceived very few. Caesar claimed to be fighting for the liberty of the people, which was being threatened by an unruly senatorial minority, for the rights of the tribunes whose veto had been suppressed and who had fled to his camp seeking protection, and for his own *dignitas* (*CW* 1.7-9). Ultimately only the last really counted. Indeed it tells us much about the value-system of the late Republic that Caesar saw fit to proclaim openly that his *dignitas* was a legitimate reason for inflicting war on his countrymen. Cicero for one was not deceived: 'And he says he is doing all for the sake of his *dignitas!*' he exclaimed, 'But where is *dignitas* without a sense of moral decency?' (*Letters to Atticus* 7.11.1).

Pompey, by contrast, claimed to be defending the authority of the senate and the honour of the Republic. It is questionable whether his motives were any purer. The cynical historian Tacitus (*Histories* 2.38) described him as 'more devious than Marius and Sulla in his quest for domination but no better'. Similarly Cassius Dio (*RH* 41.53.2), who is generally less skeptical by far, was of the opinion that both men sought to establish a monarchy.

If indeed there really was a greater justification, it lay with the supporters of Pompey, since Caesar's sole aim was to prevent his enemies from terminating his career. It is a measure of the depth of public unease at the prospect of internecine strife that practically none of Caesar's political allies signed up for the war.

As we saw earlier (ch.3), the ultimate origins of the war lay in the fact that the Republic was no longer able to function within the laws and guidelines that had been laid down for it four hundred years earlier. It is important to appreciate that this was not a war that reflected any deep division within the polity itself. Just as there were no real principles at stake, so there was little to be gained by either side except personal advantage and advancement. The grounds for the conflict were of interest primarily to the senatorial class, while the war was waged mainly by Rome's professional armies. What proportion of the non-enlisted citizen body participated is anyone's guess. Cicero claims that 'every disreputable person in Italy was with Caesar' (*Letters to Atticus* 9.19). No doubt many desperate men were attracted to both sides by extravagant promises of rewards.

Contributing to the pointlessness of the conflict was the fact that the two principal disputants were themselves reluctant to engage in hostilities. Their misfortune – and we might add Rome's tragedy – was that they found themselves on a collision course at a time when the republican system, creaking under the weight of its own inadequacies, increasingly needed one man to exercise sole control. Caesar, who had rarely consulted the senate during his years as proconsul, wanted to become master of Rome. It was a logical progression. He was the most successful general in Rome's entire history. With what authority should the senate now demand his submission? In addition – a recurring problem from the time of Marius onwards – his veterans were clamouring for land.

Once again our principal witness is Caesar himself. Even more than in his *Commentaries on the Gallic War* Caesar seeks to exaggerate the justice of his cause, notably in his description of the events leading up to the outbreak of hostilities, where he depicts himself as a thorough-going constitutionalist, 'ready to plumb any depths and put up with anything for the sake of the Republic' (*CW* 1.9).

With the benefit of hindsight it is all-too tempting to regard the Civil War as a *pro forma* exercise whose end result was never seriously in doubt. As Caesar correctly surmised at the river Rubicon, he was taking a huge gamble. More than once his troops, exhausted by the exertions of the Gallic campaign, became disaffected. Overall, they were to prove less loyal than they had done during the previous war. Despite his early successes the outcome hung in the balance on more than one occasion. Pompey's strategy was to starve Italy into submission by blocking her vital imports of corn, notably from Sicily and Sardinia. He might well have succeeded but for the energetic and unrelenting campaign which his opponent waged. Caesar had only one legion in Italy at the outset, the remaining nine being in Gaul. Pompey had the two legions recently assigned to him, though since they had formerly fought under Caesar they were hardly reliable, plus seven more legions in Spain. He also had control of the sea.

'If I stamp my foot,' Pompey grandiloquently declared, 'all Italy will rise' (Plutarch *Pompey* 57.9). Instead, as Caesar marched south, he turned and fled. He seems to have been taken completely aback by Caesar's decisiveness and rapidity of movement. So, too, in all probability was the senate, which had passed the *senatus consultum ultimum* merely to put further pressure on Caesar, rather than as a declaration of war. One after another the Italian cities opened their gates without a fight, including the region of Picenum in the north-east where Pompey had many supporters. Caesar swept south to Brundisium, where he besieged Pompey and his army as they were waiting to board ship sailing eastwards. One last effort on his part to reach a peaceful settlement was rejected. On 17th March Pompey set sail for the Balkan peninsula. Caesar, with no ships available, had no option but to turn north and enter Rome. He broke into the public treasury, appointed M. Aemilius Lepidus as prefect of the city and put Mark Antony in charge of Italy. Cicero, who had resisted Caesar's appeal to join his cause, finally left Italy to join Pompey on 7th June.

To protect his rear Caesar first led his forces to Spain, which he succeeded in taking within three months. In early August he won a decisive victory at Ilerda (Lérida) in north-east Spain. Still hopeful, perhaps, that hostilities could be nipped in the bud, he acted with exemplary clemency.

Since many of his captives had served under Pompey, he did not compel any to serve in his army against their will. He also restored their confiscated property. He then took Massilia (Marseilles), after a siege that lasted six months. Two of his legates proceeded to capture Sardinia, thereby forestalling Pompey's intention to starve Italy by means of a naval blockade. However, one of them, the former tribune C. Scribonius Curio, was caught in a trap in the province of Africa (modern Tunisia) by king Juba I of Numidia, Pompey's ally. Curio was killed and his forces massacred. Africa, which was a vital source of Rome's corn supply, was destined to remain in Pompeian hands for two and a half more years.

Caesar spent ten days in Rome holding elections and quelling a riot among his troops. Then he crossed the Adriatic in the middle of winter. He continuously dogged Pompey's steps and, after a daring night march, sought to surround him at Dyrrhachium (modern Durrës in Albania). Pompey eventually managed to break through Caesar's blockade, though he failed to follow up his success. 'Victory would today have gone to the enemy', Caesar commented, 'if they had someone who knew how to win' (Plutarch *JC* 39.5). He pursued Pompey to Thessaly in central Greece, finally confronting him in the plain of Pharsalus on 9th August. Caesar was outnumbered by more than two to one.

In the ensuing battle 15,000 Pompeians perished and only 200 Caesarians. 'This is what they willed', Caesar noted as he surveyed the carnage, transferring all the blame to the enemy. The surviving Pompeians, about 20,000 in number, surrendered to him the following day. Once again Caesar displayed clemency. Though many senators and knights were executed, men of special distinction, including M. Brutus and C. Cassius, his future assassins, were spared. Henceforth the war would grow increasingly bitter.

Following his victory, Caesar pursued Pompey to Alexandria, only to discover upon arrival in Egypt that his enemy had been murdered. This had been done on the orders of the young king Ptolemy XIII, probably as a gesture of goodwill towards Caesar. Plutarch (*JC* 48) tells us that Caesar refused to gaze upon Pompey's severed head, though he wept on being shown his signet ring, an action which furnished proof that he was dead. Lucan (*CW* 9.1038-43) pictures Caesar shedding crocodile tears to feign his unbridled delight at the death of his rival. For all we know, he may well be right. Certainly Ptolemy's action had spared Caesar the necessity, and resulting opprobrium, of carrying out a similar action himself.

With only two legions under his command Caesar intervened in the internal politics of Egypt, where a civil war was brewing over the Egyptian kingship. He also began an affair with the twenty-one year old Cleopatra VII Philopator, while being besieged in her palace by Ptolemy's army. It is alleged that Cleopatra was smuggled into the palace wrapped inside a carpet to escape detection by her brother. We do not know what attracted Caesar to Cleopatra nor indeed to what extent his decision to settle things in Egypt was prompted by his infatuation with her. By all accounts she was hardly a raving beauty (see pl. vi, c). Perhaps, as Plutarch (*Mark Antony* 27) seems to suggest, it was 'her charm, the quality of her voice, the brilliance of her conversation and her stimulating personality' which bewitched Caesar. It is claimed that Caesar accidentally set fire to the great library at Alexandria, thereby destroying one of the wonders of the ancient world and depriving the world of much ancient literature, though the report may merely be malign gossip. Eventually a relief army consisting mainly of Jews from Syria arrived to lift the siege. A fierce battle ensued, which ended in Ptolemy's death and the capture of Alexandria.

Caesar installed Cleopatra on the throne as joint-ruler with her younger brother Ptolemy XIV. Suetonius (*DJ* 52.1) claims that Caesar and the queen took a honeymoon cruise up the Nile but this may either be a later fantasy or a piece of contemporary anti-Caesarian propaganda. In June 47 he left Egypt and hastened to Syria, where Mithridates' son Pharnaces II, king of Pontus, was agitating against Roman rule. Following his victory at Zela on 1st August he succinctly declared, 'I came, I saw, I overcame.' (The alliteration – '*veni, vidi, vici*' – has particular force in Latin.) Caesar was now master of almost the entire Mediterranean.

Cleopatra meanwhile gave birth to a boy called Ptolemy XV Caesar, who was nicknamed Caesarion (little Caesar). The implication that Caesar was the father suited her political objectives. Caesar's biographer C. Oppius even went so far as to write a book demonstrating that Caesar was not the father, which proves how seriously the allegation damaged his reputation (Suetonius *DJ* 52.2). Neither his previous wife Pompeia nor his current wife Calpurnia had borne him any offspring, and though barrenness was extremely common in the ancient world, the greater likelihood is that he suffered from either a low sperm count or poor motility.

In October Caesar returned to Rome where he remained for about three months. A revolt threatened among his veterans, who were await-ing discharge and rewards for the campaign. The sources state that he quelled it simply by addressing them as '*quirites*' (citizens) instead of as 'fellow-soldiers', thereby intimating that they had forfeited their privileged military status. In December he crossed to north Africa, where the Pompeians had regrouped under the command of Pompey's son-in-law, Metellus Scipio, aided by Juba I. After inviting a blockade, Caesar routed their combined forces at Thapsus on 6th April 46. It was not a memorable victory. When the Pompeians threw down their arms in surrender, Caesar's troops, ignoring the pleas of their general and his legates, went on the rampage and massacred them. Later they turned their swords on their own officers for failing to restrain them. At the end of the day 50,000 enemy lay dead. The violence of the slaughter was an indication of the war-weary condition of Caesar's soldiers. They had no doubt bitterly come to resent his policy of clemency, which they saw as counter-productive to a swift cessation of hostilities.

Learning of their defeat from the remnant of the army, M. Porcius Cato, commander of the Pompeian garrison at Utica some fifty miles away, chose to commit suicide in preference to becoming the recipient of Caesar's clemency. He spent his last night reading Plato's dialogue the *Phaedo* on the immortality of the soul. Cato had intended to take his own life in the privacy of his own chamber but his groans alerted his slaves. His physician attempted to bandage up the wound but Cato tore off the dressing and bled to death (*African War* 88).

Cato belonged to the Greek philosophical sect founded in the third century BCE known as the Stoics. The Stoics exalted death as the guarantor of personal freedom and saw suicide as an honourable way out of an intolerable existence, whether due to physical pain, abject misery or political oppression. His death no less than his life embodied the highest principles of Stoic virtue, as governed by reason and conscience. 'I envy you your death, for you envied me the opportunity to spare you', Caesar remarked (Plutarch *Cato* 72.2). The republican cause effectively died with Cato, the most principled of Pompey's supporters.[12] Later Cicero wrote an essay entitled 'Cato', in which he lauded the dead man's achievements; in characteristic fashion Caesar sought to set the record straight by publishing a vitriolic essay entitled 'Anti-Cato'.

When Caesar returned from Africa in July 46, he went first to his country estate at Labici, a village twelve miles to the south-east of Rome. There, on 13th September, he wrote his will, the details of which are preserved by Suetonius (*DJ* 83.2), who almost certainly consulted the original in the imperial archives. In it he bequeathed three-quarters of his estate to C. Octavius, the future emperor Augustus and grandson of his sister Julia, whom he adopted in the event of his death. Velleius Paterculus (*RH* 2.59) says that Caesar loved Octavius 'as if he were his own son'. He had served as Caesar's legate in Spain, been accorded the privilege of riding beside him in his carriage and was due to serve with him again in Parthia. The remaining quarter was divided equally between another grandnephew, L. Pinarius, and a nephew, Q. Pedius, a dumb mute. Caesar designated the assassin Dec. Junius Brutus Albinus to be his secondary heir. This meant that Decimus would inherit in the event of his other heirs predeceasing him or declining their inheritance.

Early in October Caesar celebrated a quadruple triumph in honour of his victories in Gaul, Egypt, the Black Sea region and Africa. As Velleius Paterculus (*RH* 2.56) reports, each triumph had its own 'theme': citrus wood for the Gallic triumph, tortoise shell for the Egyptian triumph, acanthus wood for the Black Sea triumph, and polished silver for the Spanish triumph. The triumphal procession set off from the Circus Flaminius in the Campus Martius, entered the city via the Triumphal gate, passed through a somewhat seedy district called the Velabrum, entered the forum and made its way up to the Capitol. The vast crowd of spectators, all dressed in white, were held back by lines of legionaries. At the head came wagons bearing shields, armour and other prizes. Next came a long line of prisoners headed by the Gallic chieftain Vercingetorix, led in chains past the booing mob.

The victorious *triumphator* was conveyed in a four-horse chariot. He was dressed in a purple toga emblazoned with stars, thought to recall the type once worn by Rome's ancient kings. His face was daubed with red lead so as to resemble the statue of *Jupiter optimus maximus* (best and greatest) that stood in the temple on the Capitol. As was traditional practice, a slave travelled in the chariot beside the *triumphator*. He held a laurel wreath over his head and constantly repeated the refrain, 'remember you are mortal', to prevent him from succumbing to hubris and incurring the envy of the gods. Behind the chariot came Caesar's veterans, carrying sprays of laurel. In accordance with ancient custom, they chanted obscene songs, mocking their general's sexual accomplishments (Suetonius *DJ* 49.4, 51):

> Caesar screwed the Gauls, Nicomedes screwed Caesar.
> Caesar, who screwed the Gauls, is triumphing,
> Nicomedes, who screwed Caesar, is not.

And:

> Citizens, guard your wives. We're escorting the bald
>   whoremonger.
> In Gaul you fucked away the gold you borrowed in Rome.

Not all went as planned. When Caesar's chariot drew level with the Temple of Fortuna, the axle broke – a very bad omen. He sought to atone for the portent, or at least to alleviate the public disquiet that it caused, by climbing the steps to the Capitol on his knees. The celebrations concluded with a huge sacrifice. Then, probably around dusk, Vercingetorix was

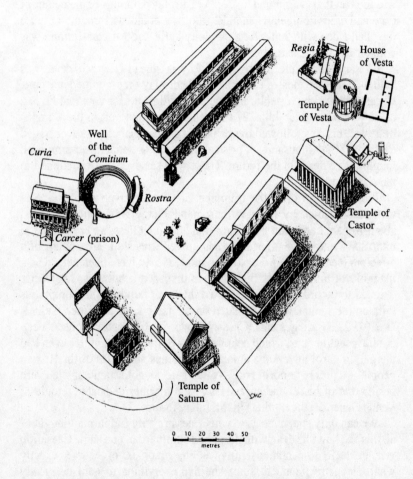

Fig. 7 The Roman Forum, reconstruction

garrotted in a stinking underground cell, in the *carcer* (the prison, see fig. 7) access to which could be gained only by a hole in the roof.

The Egyptian triumph was remarkable for the inclusion of Cleopatra's sister Arsinoë among the captives, since customarily the Romans refrained from exhibiting women in chains. The African triumph caused even graver offence. As Romans could not legally triumph over fellow Romans, Caesar claimed a victory over King Juba I of Numidia. Juba had perished in battle, so the crowd was treated to the spectacle of his four-year-old son being paraded in his place. What really incensed the *plebs*, however, was the fact that Caesar had his soldiers display paintings of the deaths of Cato and other Pompeian generals, whom he branded as traitors because they had sided with Juba. As a publicity gaffe, the African triumph was without equal in Caesar's career.

Caesar's quadruple triumph, which was spread over ten days, was without doubt the most spectacular public display ever mounted in Rome. It was followed by a public banquet, in fulfilment of a vow that he had made to his daughter Julia. 22,000 tables were laid out on the Campus Martius. This was followed by the largest gladiatorial contest ever staged in Rome. Many thousands of prisoners, as well as condemned criminals, fought to the death in the forum. Those who survived were auctioned in the slave markets.

Probably soon after the triumphs Cleopatra arrived in Rome. She was accompanied by her new husband Ptolemy XIV, who was aged about fifteen, her infant son Caesarion and, doubtless, a very large and impressive entourage. Her entry has proved irresistible to modern film directors (see p. 110 f.). For all we know, it may have been staged as a magnificent finale to the triumphs that preceded it but, if so, no writer deigned to record it. Caesar installed the royal family in his sumptuous villa on the Janiculan hill, situated on the far side of the Tiber. Cassius Dio (43.27.3) alleges that Caesar's love for Cleopatra aroused deep public resentment, to which he remained wholly indifferent. He even had the gall to enrol the couple among the 'friends and allies of the Roman people' – a purely honorific title – and to erect a gold statue of Cleopatra beside that of his divine ancestress in the recently dedicated temple of Venus Genetrix (the mother) in the Julian forum.

We can only speculate as to what Caesar's wife Calpurnia thought of all this and how she dealt with the public humiliation. The name Caesarion was in itself a scandalous provocation, which is, of course, exactly what Cleopatra intended, since she had everything to gain politically by boasting of her liaison with the dictator. Did she perhaps nag him to adopt her son and, if so, did this cause tension in their relationship?

Certainly Cleopatra's presence played directly into the hands of Caesar's enemies, who put it about that he not only intended to divorce Calpurnia, marry the oriental queen and legitimise Caesarion, but also to transfer the capital from Rome to Alexandria. Very likely the loathing that the Roman people felt towards the Egyptian queen contributed significantly to the conspirators' belief that Caesar's death would be greeted with popular rejoicing and relief.

Even now, among all these celebrations, peace remained for Caesar as elusive as ever. In November he hurriedly left for Spain to quell a revolt by Pompey's sons, Gnaeus and Sextus, who had succeeded in raising a force of thirteen legions. As Spain was where hostilities had commenced four years ago, Caesar may well have experienced a discomforting sense of *déjà vu*. According to the Christian writer Orosius (6.16.6), who lived in the fifth century CE, Caesar covered the 1100 miles from Rome to Saguntum (just north of modern Valencia) in only seventeen days. Strabo (3.4.9), who lived in the reign of Augustus, alleges that he traversed the remaining 250 miles to his military headquarters at Obulco in another ten days. This would mean he averaged over fifty miles per day – an impossible accomplishment. We can at any rate assume that he arrived with lightning speed. He described the march in a lost poem called 'The Journey', which he found time to compose along the way.

The decisive battle, one of the toughest in Caesar's career, was fought at Munda (perhaps modern Urso) on 17th March. 'Caesar has often fought for victory but never before for his own skin', he remarked afterwards (Plutarch *JC* 56.3). Following the defeat of the Pompeians, Gnaeus was hunted down and killed. Sextus escaped to fight another day. Though he posed no further threat to Caesar, he was destined to become a thorn in the side of Mark Antony and Octavian for many years to come. During his stay in Spain Caesar began planning a campaign against Parthia (corresponding approximately to Iran) in order, as we have seen, to avenge the defeat of Crassus at the battle of Carrhae.

Throughout the Civil War Caesar was concerned to legalise his position, conscious that Pompey's claim to have been acting constitutionally throughout his career was much stronger than his. He tried to solve his dilemma by repeatedly holding the consulship and, ever more frequently, the dictatorship. In 49 he became dictator for only eleven days, primarily for the purpose of holding elections in Rome. In 48 he held his second consulship. Following his victory at Pharsalus, he was appointed dictator for a year with an unspecified charge. He was consul for the third time in 46. When news of his victory at Thapsus reached the senate he was elected dictator for ten years, probably 'for settling the Republic' (*rei publicae constituendae*), a conveniently vague and open-ended commission that left him free to interpret his office as he saw fit. As had been the case during Caesar's proconsulship, Balbus and Oppius conducted business on his behalf in Rome. Neither held any official position and both were answerable exclusively to Caesar.

Caesar passed, or at least planned, more reforms than any of his predecessors. They included (and this is by no means a complete list): the reduction of the number of corn dole recipients in Rome from 300,000 to 160,000; the settling of the surplus population of Rome in shortly-to-be-founded colonies; the suppression of what he deemed to be 'illegal' foreign religious associations (he exempted the Jews from his ban); the building of a large artificial harbour at Rome's port of Ostia to facilitate super-cargoes carrying grain; the codification of the laws; an increase in the number of magistracies; the draining of marshes to extend the amount of agricultural land that was available near Rome; the introduction of sumptuary laws to check extravagant waste; the construction of a number of new buildings, most notably the Julian forum; and the standardisation of the municipal administration of Italy.

Not the least of Caesar's accomplishments was his reform of the calendar. The practice of intercalation had been neglected in the years leading up to the Civil War, with the consequence that by 46 the calendrical year was well over two months behind the solar year. Caesar remedied the situation temporarily by intercalating two months between November and December, in addition to having intercalated a third in February, making a total of 445 days. It was, he declared, 'the last year of confusion'. On 1st January 45 Caesar introduced the solar calendar of 365.25 days (see further p. 95). Even this achievement was treated with scorn by his detractors. When someone observed that the constellation of Lyra was due to rise the following evening, Cicero tartly observed, 'yes, by order of Caesar' (Plutarch *JC* 59.3).

What Caesar did not do either during the Civil War or in his final year was to tackle the pressing question of constitutional reform.

Chapter 7

The Final Months

Caesar returned home from Spain a conquering hero in October 45. Less than six months later he was assassinated. What happened in those final months to fuel such hatred? Did his personality undergo a sea-change? Or had his domination in itself become intolerable?

The Caesar of the final months provides a fascinating case-study for anyone interested in the effects of absolute power upon the personality. He no longer placed any stock by his public image. On the contrary, he seems almost to have set about wilfully to deface it. Time and again his actions reveal a disregard for public opinion, as if he was trying to see just how far he could go in alienating both the populace and his peers. Literary sources suggest that his health was in decline, and this is also indicated by his portraits on coins. A year or so before Caesar's death Cicero in one of his lawcourt speeches (*in defence of Marcellus* 25) quotes him as saying that he had 'lived long enough whether one measures life in length of years or in the attainment of *gloria*'. He further reports (*Letters to Atticus* 13.52) that when Caesar visited his country estate four months before his death he was following a course of emetics. It would hardly be surprising if Caesar was suffering from physical and mental exhaustion. After twelve years sleeping rough he must have looked incredibly weather-beaten. Though we hear of no serious injuries · he probably had numerous battle scars. He may also have been troubled by war wounds. Doubtless, too, there were dark shadows under his eyes from overwork. His teeth – any, that is, which remained – were probably blackened, carious and worn down to the stumps.

It is also evident that Caesar had grown intolerant of opposition, impatient of the necessary formalities and protocols that are embedded in any governmental system, and, as we would say today, given to violent mood swings. All these characteristics were accentuated by his fits of epilepsy, the first of which, as documented by Plutarch (*JC* 17.3), occurred in Spain at the beginning of the Civil War. Our sources are oddly silent about the impact of these fits upon his public image. Shakespeare (*Julius Caesar* Act I Scene 2) suggests that it was Caesar's feebleness, contrasting so markedly with his arrogant demeanour, that particularly repelled Cassius, but this is pure supposition. Nor do we know whether Caesar himself was troubled by the fear of succumbing to a fit in public. The honours that the senate heaped upon him in his final months may have accentuated an innate tendency towards megalomania. Despite the senate's subservience, he probably felt unappreciated and misunderstood. He was surely aware that his achievements had aroused as much envy as admiration among his peers. That he had some inkling of his unpopularity is indicated by an off-hand remark which he made to an ex-praetor called Publius Sestius: 'I should be an idiot to suppose that even an affable fellow like Cicero is my friend when he has to wait upon my convenience', which Cicero quotes a month after his death (*Letters to Atticus* 14.2). It is probable, too, that Caesar had succumbed to the atmosphere of oriental pomp and luxury that surrounded him in Egypt and that this in turn influenced how he expected to be treated. Lastly, he may have felt that he was fading both physically and psychologically.

Like the African triumph before it, the Spanish triumph turned out to be a political disaster. Caesar was once again using the occasion to commemorate a victory over his Pompeian adversaries. This time one of Rome's senior magistrates registered his displeasure in a very public way. When Caesar's triumphal chariot rolled past the platform alongside the Sacred Way where the tribunes of the *plebs* all stood to attention, one of their number, Pontius Aquila, resolutely remained seated. Caesar was incandescent with rage. For the next few days he concluded all his statements with the sardonic observation, 'that is, of course, if Pontius Aquila has no objection' (Suetonius *DJ* 78.2).

Possibly for health reasons, possibly due to overwork, Caesar resigned from his sole consulship shortly afterwards. He handed over the office to two of his former legates, Q. Fabius Maximus, a descendant of the famous dictator (see p. 17) and C. Trebonius. This, too, caused grave offence, since it smacked of disrespect for the republican constitution. Suetonius informs us that when Maximus was first introduced to the people at the theatre by a *lictor* (an official who preceded a senior magistrate carrying a bundle of rods and axes known as *fasces* as a symbol of the magistrate's authority), the crowd denounced him for not being a proper consul.

The final months of Caesar's life proceed with an inexorable momentum. On 18th December, while staying with his niece and her husband in Puteoli (Pozzuoli) on the Bay of Naples, he visited Cicero, accompanied by a bodyguard of 2,000 Spanish soldiers. On the last day of the year, while presiding over the election of quaestors in the *comitia tributa* (tribal assembly), he received news that the consul Q.

Fabius Maximus had died. He hastily summoned the *comitia centuriata* (centuriate assembly) and supervised the election of an ex-legate named C. Caninius Rebilus, who then served for less than one day. This caused Cicero (*Letters to Friends* 7.30) to quip that Rebilus was a wonderfully wide-awake consul, since he did not once fall asleep during his entire period of office. The next day Caesar entered on his fifth consulship with Mark Antony as his colleague. He immediately announced that when he departed for the east in March, he would hand over his consulship to P. Cornelius Dolabella, Cicero's son-in-law. This did not sit well with Mark Antony, who threatened to use his power as an *augur* or priestly diviner to obstruct Dolabella's election. Nor did it sit well with the people, who once again saw Caesar treating the consulship as an old shoe, to be put on and discarded at will. Caesar also nominated consuls for the next two years, A. Hirtius and C. Vibius Pansa for 43, and Dec. Brutus and L. Munatius Plancus for 42. This shows that he was expecting the war in Parthia to be protracted.

Caesar's increasing inability to control his temper was starkly revealed on 26th January at the Latin Festival. This ancient festival, one of Rome's most important, commemorated the unification of Latium. It was celebrated outside Rome on the Alban Mount, the site of Alba Longa, which according to tradition had been founded by Aeneas' son Ascanius, otherwise known as Iulus. As Caesar entered the forum on his return from the festival amid enthusiastic displays of public support, someone ran forward and crowned his statue with a laurel wreath to which a white fillet had been attached. This, the traditional emblem of Persian royalty, was also used by kings in the Greek-speaking world and its symbolism would have been instantly recognizable to the crowd of onlookers.

When two tribunes called Epidius Marullus and Caesetius Flavus ordered that the diadem be removed and the culprit led off to prison, Caesar immediately stripped them of their office with a harsh reprimand. His action was variously interpreted in antiquity. Nicolaus of Damascus (Fragment 130.69) maintains that he was angry with the tribunes for failing to prevent the man from placing the diadem on his statue. Suetonius (*DJ* 79), by contrast, alleges that he was upset 'either because the intimation of royal power had met with such little success or, as he himself claimed, because the glory of refusing it had been denied to him'. He continues: 'henceforth he was unable to dissociate himself from the invidious impression of seeking the kingship, even though, when the people hailed him as king, he replied, "I am not king but Caesar"'. This was in effect a rather feeble play on words, since '*rex*' (king), like '*Caesar*', was a traditional Roman *cognomen* (see note 5).

At an unknown date the senate met in Caesar's absence and bestowed upon him a profusion of unparalleled honours. These included dictator for life, prefect of morals for life, and the purely honorific title *parens* or *pater patriae* (parent or father of his country). The month Quinctilis was to be renamed Julius (July). On all public occasions he was entitled to sit on a gilded chair, wear a triumphal robe and sport a laurel crown. His birthday was to be a public holiday. All the magistrates took an oath to defend his acts and the senators to defend his person. If he fathered a son, that son was automatically to be appointed supreme pontiff in the event of his death. Suetonius (*DJ* 77), quoting a supporter of Pompey, tells us that Sulla's resignation from the dictatorship prompted Caesar to observe that 'Sulla did not know his political ABC'. Conceivably he made the remark shortly before or after becoming dictator for life, in order to quash any hope that he would follow Sulla's lead.

Cassius Dio (*RH* 44.6) states, 'finally the senators addressed him explicitly as Jupiter Julius and they decreed that a temple be dedicated to him and his *clementia*'. Likewise Appian (*CW* 2.106) writes: 'the senate decreed the erection of many temples to him as a god, and one jointly to him and Clemency, in which the two were represented clasping hands'. Caesar was not yet a god – that would come later – but the process was well under way. He had already been identified with a specific god and a distinctive attribute of his, his clemency, was now regarded as divine. The practice of awarding divine honours to human beings originated with the Greeks, though ancestor worship no doubt played its part in further accommodating the Romans to the concept. Divine honours had been bestowed upon a number of Roman generals by grateful provincials out in the East. However, the award of divine honours to a living man by the Roman senate was a different matter altogether. Both Plutarch and Cassius Dio suggest that the intention behind the proposal was to stir up ill-will towards Caesar. But if that is the case, how is it that Caesar was hoodwinked?

According to Suetonius, the incident which caused most ill-will occurred when the senate, headed by Mark Antony, approached him with a copy of the decrees about honours which they had just awarded him, while he was seated before the temple of Venus Genetrix in the Julian Forum. Plutarch (*JC* 60) alleges that he was 'very eager to rise before the senate but, as the story goes, one of his friends or rather one of his flatterers, Cornelius Balbus, restrained him with the words, "remember that you are Caesar. Do you not think it right that you are courted as a superior?"'. In other words, both writers suggest that the insult was unintended. Caesar later sent word that he had not been feeling well. Did he perhaps remain seated to disguise an attack of diarrhoea?

On 15th February, at the festival known as the Lupercalia, Caesar appeared for the first time in the ceremonial dress of a Roman king. The Lupercalia, whose name derives from the *lupus* (wolf) which suckled the infants Romulus and Remus, was a festival of purification and fertility. It perhaps survives today in a watered-down version through rituals associated with St Valentine. Half-naked priests known as *Luperci*, clad only in a wolf-mask and loincloth, ran round the Palatine Hill, striking the hands of all the women whom they encountered with straps made of goat's hide to promote their fertility. Caesar observed the ceremony while seated on the rostra, the speakers' platform in the forum.[13]

At the end of the run Antony, who was one of the Luperci, ascended the rostra and offered Caesar a diadem tied with a wreath of laurel. Plutarch tells us that this was greeted by some pre-arranged clapping. However, when Caesar thrust it away the entire gathering burst into applause. When Antony offered him the wreath a second time, again a few people clapped and, when he declined it for the second time, again the whole crowd applauded. 'As the experiment had not succeeded,' Plutarch concludes, 'Caesar rose from his seat and ordered that the wreath be carried to the Capitol' (*JC* 61.4).

The significance of this incident has been variously interpreted from antiquity onwards. Was it a fake coronation orchestrated by Caesar, who was acting in cahoots with Mark Antony? And if so, was it his purpose to test the waters of popular opinion or, alternatively, to dispel the rumour that he was aiming at kingship by publicly declining the offer? Or was the charade devised by Caesar's enemies to stir up the people against him and to make them better disposed towards his assassination? And if so, did Antony go along with them in the knowledge that it was intended to make Caesar unpopular or was he similarly duped?

Cicero later alleged that it was this incident which made Mark Antony the real murderer, whereas Plutarch, as we have seen, assumes that it was an 'experiment' on Caesar's part, intended to determine the level of public support for his establishment as king.

The Lupercalia is our last definite sighting of Caesar prior to his murder. Very little is known of the final month of his life. He had now reached the pinnacle of his career. He was dictator in perpetuity and his word was law. What other honours, beside the offer of kingship, could be strewn in his path? He presumably remained in Rome, pre-occupied with arrangements for his departure for Parthia. Maybe he spent his days on the Campus Martius, engaged in military exercises. He was after all assembling a larger force than any which he had previously taken into the field – 10,000 horse and no fewer than sixteen legions, six of which were spending the winter in Apollonia on the west coast of Greece with Octavius. In addition to the usual administrative chores, Caesar was also taking a personal interest in his ambitious public works program. In his spare moments he probably diverted himself in the company of Cleopatra.

Around the middle of February Caesar was accosted in the street by a seer called Spurinna, who in the words of Valerius Maximus (8.11.2), a writer living in the reign of the emperor Tiberius, warned him 'to beware of the next thirty days, the last of which was the ides of March, on the grounds that they were deadly'.

On 1st March the election of the consuls and tribunes took place in the *comitia centuriata*. About the same time Caesar increased the membership of the senate from 600 to 900. He did so partly to reward those who had proved their loyalty to him in the Gallic and Civil Wars and partly to deal with increased administrative demands. The new senators included centurions and sons of freedmen from all over Italy. Caesar's move deeply offended the Roman nobility, who made laboured jokes at the expense of the new men. For instance, a notice was posted in the city stating, 'let no-one give directions as to the whereabouts of the senate house to any new senator.'

At some point probably in the final month of his life Caesar dismissed his Spanish bodyguard. The reason why he did so is unclear. Did he put confidence in the oath of loyalty that the senate and magistrates had taken earlier? Did he rely on the support and protection of the common people? Did he suspect that his bodyguard was contributing to his unpopularity? Or had he merely grown indifferent to life?

Whatever the explanation, it was a fateful decision and it may well have been this action which convinced the conspirators, a cowardly consortium, that they had nothing to fear by taking his life.

Chapter 8

The Conspiracy

It has been aptly remarked that no secret was better kept. Nicolaus of Damascus claims there were 'more than eighty' conspirators, whereas Suetonius puts the number at 'more than sixty'. Even the lower figure tells us worlds about Caesar's isolation. We know of twenty of the conspirators by name. Seven had supported Caesar in the Civil War, nine sided with Pompey, and four are of unknown allegiance. Seneca (*on Anger* 3.30.4), claimed that more friends than enemies joined the conspiracy.

C. Cassius Longinus was almost certainly the instigator of the plan to assassinate Caesar. Cassius had been Crassus' quaestor on his disastrous expedition against the Parthians. After Crassus' death and defeat at Carrhae, Cassius escaped to Syria, which he successfully defended. He was tribune of the *plebs* in the year that the Civil War broke out. He sided with Pompey and commanded a fleet in the Adriatic. Like many of the assassins, he was pardoned by Caesar after the battle of Pharsalus. Caesar subsequently appointed him praetor in charge of lawsuits involving non-citizens for 44 and designated him consul for 41. Even so, Cassius felt aggrieved, since he coveted the senior praetorship that Caesar bestowed upon his co-conspirator Marcus Brutus.

Plutarch (*JC* 62; *Brutus* 8.2) claims that Caesar mistrusted Cassius' pale complexion and slight build – features, incidentally, that he shared with Brutus. Cassius was 'a hot-headed man who hated Caesar more for private reasons than for public ones, and was the one who incited Brutus'. Whereas 'Brutus objected to the rule, Cassius objected to the ruler'. A portrait head depicting a man with lean cheeks, thin lips and a ruthless mouth, may be that of Cassius (pl. iv).

Some time in the second half of January 45 Cassius wrote to Cicero, stating that he 'preferred to have an old and forgiving master' – meaning Caesar – 'than to try a new, cruel one' – meaning Pompey's son Sextus (Cicero, *Letters to Friends* 19.4). Only six weeks later he had changed his mind. Married to Brutus' half-sister Junia Tertulla, Cassius was thirty-eight.

Cassius knew that if the murder was to gain popular acceptance, he had to win the support of M. Junius Brutus, a man widely respected among the Roman élite both as a rhetorician and as a philosopher (pl. viii, a). Cicero greatly admired Brutus and had dedicated several of his philosophical works to him, including a dialogue entitled *Brutus* that celebrated his rhetorical powers. Caesar, too, admired his eloquence and once commented when Brutus pleaded before him, 'I have no idea what the man wants but, whatever it is, he wants it very much' (Cicero *Letters to Friends* 14.1).

Brutus' credentials made him an ideal co-conspirator. His mother was Servilia, Caesar's one-time mistress and Cato's half-sister. He had actually been educated by Cato, who had no doubt indoctrinated him into his sullen and diehard republican principles. Cicero's friend and correspondent T. Pomponius Atticus had drawn up Brutus' family tree, in which he traced his descent on his father's side from L. Junius Brutus, who had expelled the last king of Rome, Tarquinius Superbus, and so inaugurated the Republic; and on his mother's side from C. Servilius Ahala, the assassin of Spurius Maelius, who was suspected of seeking to establish a monarchy by bribing the masses with gifts of corn. The stemma of his family was prominently displayed on the wall of Brutus' private office.

Brutus, who was deeply influenced by Platonic philosophy, committed himself to the conspiracy partly because he believed that its aims conformed to the principles of Plato's *Republic* (8.564a), in which it is stated that 'tyranny is the worst kind of servitude'.[14] It is questionable whether he deserves the accolade 'the noblest Roman of them all', which Mark Antony bestows upon him in Shakespeare's play – questionable, too, for that matter, whether Shakespeare's Antony sincerely means it – though it should not be doubted that Brutus' motives for killing Caesar were primarily ideological.

Though Brutus supported Pompey in the Civil War, this fact had in no way diminished Caesar's regard for him. Caesar may also have felt continuing affection for Brutus' mother. After the battle of Pharsalus he had ordered a special search for Brutus, fearful that he might be among the dead. He had appointed him urban (i.e. senior) praetor in charge of lawsuits involving citizens. Brutus, who was about forty, was married to Cato's niece Porcia. Porcia was the ex-wife of M. Calpurnius Bibulus, Caesar's unco-operative colleague in his consulship of 59. They were a devoted pair, so much so that Brutus revealed to his wife the details of the plot after she had detected his troubled aspect. So far as we know, she was the only woman privy to the conspiracy.

Cassius' initial approach to Brutus was unsuccessful. Shortly afterwards, however, the latter happened to visit a close friend called Q.

Ligarius. Plutarch (*Brutus* 11) tells us that Brutus found Ligarius ill in bed
and said to him teasingly, 'this is a fine time to be sick'. Ligarius raised
himself up on his elbow and, grasping his friend by the hand, replied, 'if
you have anything in mind worthy of yourself, Brutus, I'm a cured man'.
The previous year Ligarius had been successfully defended by Cicero
against a charge of treason brought against him by Caesar and had been
permitted to return from exile. He probably resented being on the receiving
end of Caesar's clemency.

In democratic spirit Brutus and Cassius agreed to exercise joint
leadership. This policy was not conducive to the success of their
operation and, as we shall see, led to some fatal errors of judgement.
We do not know exactly when they began to make approaches to the
others but, given the risk of discovery, they probably held off till the last
possible moment. Suetonius (*JC* 80) states that the final decision was
made only after Caesar had called a meeting of the senate for the *ides*
of March.[15] Very likely he made that announcement on the *kalends* (first
day) of March, since the senate regularly met on the kalends of each
month.

The most valuable of their recruits was Dec. Junius Brutus Albinus,
a distant relative of M. Brutus. No-one had received more favour from
Caesar than Decimus. He had been a senior legate in the Gallic and Civil
Wars and was currently serving as praetor. Caesar had nominated him to
be propraetor of Cisalpine Gaul for 44-3 and consul for 42. As we have
seen (p. 52), Caesar trusted Decimus so much that he had made him his
secondary heir; it would add much to our insight into his character if we
knew whether Decimus had been informed of this fact. Plutarch alleges
that he was asked to join 'not as a man who had much initiative or daring,
but since he was powerful both because of the large number of gladiators
whom he was supervising for the Roman games and because Caesar trusted
him' (*Brutus* 12.5). He certainly played a pivotal role in the conspiracy.
Not only did he accompany Caesar to dinner the night before the murder
but he also overcame Caesar's reluctance to attend the senate the following
morning. Married to Cassius' daughter, Decimus was thirty-five. Another
former legate of Caesar who joined the conspiracy was C. Trebonius. He
had served as tribune of the *plebs* in 55, praetor in 48, governor of Further
Spain in 47-46, and suffect (i.e. replacement) consul in 45.

There were others who felt that their talents had gone unrecognised.
One was L. Minucius Basilus, who had served as a praetor in 45 but not
been assigned a provincial governorship. Another was Serv. Sulpicius
Galba, praetor in 54, who had also been passed over. To increase his
discomfort, Galba was financially indebted to Caesar. He had stood as

guarantor for Pompey when the latter had borrowed heavily from Caesar. Though Caesar had never demanded repayment, Galba may have found it intolerable living with the possibility that one day he might. Prominent among the Pompeians was Pontius Aquila, the tribune of the *plebs* who had had the temerity to remain seated when Caesar rode by him during his Spanish triumph.

Though it is extremely unlikely whether any approach was made to Mark Antony (pl. v) or M. Lepidus, the master of horses (see p. 48), there was much discussion about whether to include Cicero. Whereas M. Brutus argued that his support would lend an air of ideological respectability to their crime, Cassius said that Cicero had too many 'scruples'. Cicero was, moreover, 59 years of age – almost a generation older than most of the conspirators. We may also doubt whether he would have agreed to participate had he been approached. 'O name him not,' says Brutus in Shakespeare's play, 'he will not follow anything that other men begin.' As he confessed in his correspondence (*Letters to Friends* 6.14.1), 'if anyone in the world is pusillanimous in important matters involving a risk…I am that man'. So they left him out.

Cicero and Caesar had known each other all their lives, and although they had often found themselves on opposite sides of the political divide, they had maintained the appearance of cordiality. Caesar greatly admired Cicero for his literary accomplishments and had dedicated his book *on Analogy* to him. He had lent him 800,000 sesterces, a debt which Cicero, over-extended financially, had never repaid. While returning from Spain, Caesar had taken time to write a letter of condolence on the occasion of his daughter's death and, as we have seen, visited him at his villa in Puteoli (Pozzuoli) near Naples a few months before his death.

Although Cicero did not himself wield a dagger on the ides of March, he may justifiably be regarded as an accomplice after the fact. He had long been flattering Marcus Brutus' vanity by extending to him a role in history equal to that of his illustrious 'tyrannicidal' ancestors. Equally revealing, Cicero began referring to Caesar as *rex* in his private correspondence from August 45 onwards. Nor did Cicero deny Mark Antony's claim that Brutus shouted out his name when he raised his dagger to stab Caesar – presumably because this was an established fact (*Philippics* 2.28).

Moreover, there can be little doubt that Cicero bore Caesar a personal grudge, in part because the latter had far exceeded his own somewhat mediocre political achievements (*Letters to his Brother Quintus* 3.5.4). But although Cicero gloated after the murder, it is questionable whether he actually wanted Caesar dead.[16] Though he adamantly denied Antony's charge that he was privy to the plot, his absence from the senate on the ides

Plate v. Antony

[a] Julius Caesar

[b] Antony

[c] Cleopatra

Plate vi

of March is somewhat curious. Conceivably the conspirators advised him to stay at home for his own good but without actually explaining why.

Brutus and Cassius rejected at least two schemes. One was to assassinate Caesar while he was strolling along the Sacred Way. Another was to throw him off the temporary bridge that was put up in the Campus Martius for the populace to cross before casting its votes in the consular elections. They probably rejected these plans in part because the response of the bystanders would have been unpredictable. Caesar's popularity had declined sharply in recent months but not to the extent that they could expect his murder to win immediate approval from the *plebs*.

The plan they eventually agreed upon was the brainchild of Cassius, who suggested that they should assassinate Caesar in the *curia* of Pompey two days before he was scheduled to leave for Parthia (see fig. 8, p. 73). They could conceal their daggers in the voluminous folds of their togas. The venue had several advantages. First, the victim would be killed away from the public gaze. Second, instead of dying at the hands of hired killers, he would die at the hands of his peers. Third, the *curia* would lend their crime a kind of legitimacy, by suggesting that it was the will of the senate. That is one of the reasons why Brutus and Cassius implicated so many in the conspiracy; presumably another was the principle of 'safety in numbers'.

The location was also extremely apt. Though any consecrated space in Rome could serve for a meeting of the senate, the *curia* of Pompey had become popular following the burning down of its counterpart in the forum. Moreover, Caesar had recently rescinded a dictat passed during the Civil War which had required the removal of all Pompey's images from public places and they had now been reinstated (Plutarch *Cicero* 40). So the victim would fall at the base of his enemy's statue. No doubt, too, some of the assassins would invoke Pompey's spirit while they were committing the murder. There was yet one further advantage to this scheme. A band of gladiators owned by Dec. Brutus, which was scheduled to perform in the adjoining theatre while the senate was in session, would, if necessary, be able to perform the function of a bodyguard.

The motives of the individual conspirators were doubtless as diverse as the men. Though a few, most notably Brutus, were fired up by the idealistic notion of ridding Rome of a hated tyrant, the majority were driven by more ignoble passions, including jealousy, hatred, fear, insecurity, ambition, and – last but not least – a sense of injured pride. Since there was a generation gap between the victim and his assassins, many of the latter may well have felt infantilised by Caesar's dismissive treatment of them. Brutus in particular may have been uncomfortable at being on the receiving end of Caesar's condescension, all the more so because of his mother's affair with the dictator.

Would some of us have identified with the conspirators and their grievances? Very likely. Would some of us have seen murder as the only way out? Possibly. The violent removal of a headstrong magistrate was hardly an unprecedented event, least of all in the late Republic. Indeed the Republic owed its origins to the overthrow of a despotic ruler. Violence was thus part of the Republic's foundation charter. Clearly the conspirators were eager to demonstrate that Caesar was a '*tyrannos*' – a Greek word meaning an illegitimate ruler. A *tyrannos* was a cruel and cynical despot who scorned constitutional principle, courted the mob, treated his peers with disdain, surrounded himself with flatterers, and sacrificed the welfare of the state to his own political advancement. This was Caesar, as they might have said, in a nutshell.

Even the mere appearance of autocracy is invidious in most governmental systems and the Roman fear of autocracy was visceral. Many moderates, even if they did not go so far as to rejoice in Caesar's murder, would have conceded that the victim 'had it coming to him'. He had done nothing to placate his enemies, even if he was ultimately innocent of the charge of seeking the crown. His relationship with Cleopatra, despite the fact that it receives little attention in our sources, caused widespread offence. Like all peoples of their time, the Romans regarded other races as inferior and the presence in their midst of a foreign queen who was claiming special privileges must have been intolerable. An allegation that the keeper of the Sibylline oracles (collections, that is, of prophetic texts) had discovered an oracle indicating that Parthia could only be conquered by a king was undoubtedly part of the smear campaign intended to discredit Caesar after his death, since it provided him with a motive for establishing a monarchy.

All this said, the difficulty in forming a balanced estimate of the murder is compounded by the fact that it was so mean-spirited and, as we shall see, so poorly executed. It is almost impossible to decide whether one feels more contempt for those who drew their knives against a brave general under whose standards they had fought in two long wars, or for those who killed a merciful opponent who had spared their lives and advanced their careers.

To mount a conspiracy involving a minimum of sixty people is a formidable undertaking, particularly since some must have been approached who did not join up. And yet no-one, it seems, blew the whistle. This is all the more remarkable in view of the fact that the conspirators did not take an oath 'in the name of all the gods and goddesses', swearing themselves to secrecy. They presumably refrained on the grounds that they were 'honourable and patriotic citizens' (see p. 81). The less dishonourable might well have concluded that it would not have amounted to much anyway, since they had recently sworn to protect the victim's life with their own. Very likely, as Plutarch (*Brutus* 12) suggests, Brutus, as a philosopher, sounded out his friends by putting to them hypothetical questions which had a practical bearing on the subject at hand. One such question might be, 'would it be just to kill a tyrant in order to restore political freedom?'. We hear of at least two potential recruits whom he rejected on the basis of their unsatisfactory answers to his questions.

Finally, Cassius recommended that Mark Antony should be assassinated along with Caesar. Brutus, however, opposed the suggestion on the grounds that his murder would detract from the 'legitimacy' of their deed. This was his first blunder; more would follow.

Chapter 9

The Murder

The 'murder of Caesar' forms a separable unit within Caesarian biography. Plutarch, Suetonius, Appian and Cassius Dio have all left us detailed accounts. Nicolaus of Damascus gives a much abbreviated description, while Velleius Paterculus passes up the opportunity altogether. In some places our authors show an almost verbatim similarity. In addition, they pepper their narrative with details that seem designed to contribute to the reader's suspense, as does their inclusion of several lines of dialogue.

Caesar's assassination is not only one of the best documented murders of all time but also the only event in the whole of Roman antiquity that we can reconstruct on an almost hour-by-hour basis. At the same time it raises a number of puzzling questions. Firstly, who supplied the evidence? After all, none of the authors who are our sources witnessed the crime. Secondly, what function did the narrative play within the tradition of pro-Caesarian and anti-Caesarian propaganda? Clearly both sides had much to make out of it. Thirdly, how much of the received narrative is historically reliable and how much is palpably fictitious? Fourthly, what is its genre? Should it be interpreted in the style of a Greek tragedy, intended to prove either that fate is inescapable or that Caesar was so over-burdened with hubris that he wilfully ignored all warnings? 'Surely we must detect the hand of all-powerful fate in all these events,' states Nicolaus of Damascus (Fragment 130.23). 'The power of the fates is inescapable,' observes Velleius Paterculus (*RH* 2.57). 'It was destined that Caesar should meet his destined end,' comments Appian (*CW* 116). Or is it an early example of a crime thriller, with the emphasis primarily upon missed signals? My own reconstruction is necessarily somewhat suppositious, drawing as it does from all the sources.

Certainly the 'murder of Caesar' reads very much like a modern suspense-story, stiff with clues as to how the crime might have been averted. Instead of clues, however, we have omens – virtually every type of omen known to the ancients – flights of birds, sickly entrails, off-hand remarks by the victim that mean more than the victim realises, dreams, fire that does not burn, thunder and lightning, warnings from seers,

71

prodigies such as weeping horses, and prophetic texts.

The ides of March, which fell on the fifteenth day of the month, were not in themselves ill-fated. On this day the urban *plebs* picnicked in a grove at the first milestone outside the Flaminian Gate on the north side of the city, near the modern Borghese Gardens and Porta del Popolo. There they celebrated Anna Perenna, the personification of the year, by singing bawdy songs and consuming as many cups of wine as each of them hoped to attain in years. It has been suggested that this was another reason why the conspirators chose this day to assassinate Caesar, since on learning of the crime the *plebs* would have been in no condition to intervene. However, there is no mention of the festivities in any of our accounts.

* * * * *

Caesar spent the day before his death in the company of M. Lepidus, master of horses,[17] attending the *equirria*, a horse-racing festival that was held in the Campus Martius. The *equirria*, which marked the beginning of the campaigning season, provided an opportunity for the cavalry to be put through its paces. Towards dusk Caesar returned to Lepidus' house for dinner. He was accompanied by Dec. Brutus, charged no doubt with the task of detecting whether Caesar suspected that his life was in danger and, if he did, of warning the co-conspirators. It was no doubt a sober, even somewhat sombre affair. Caesar was not a heavy drinker and Lepidus was hardly the life and soul of the party. Decimus' unease must have added to the tension. Yet if Caesar detected anything, he kept it to himself. In fact he occupied himself by signing letters, as was his custom when in company. However, when the topic of conversation turned to the question, 'What is the best way to die?', he looked up from his papers and without a moment's hesitation replied, 'Unexpectedly' (Plutarch *JC* 63.4).

5 a.m.

Well before dawn the conspirators assembled at Cassius' house and accompanied him to the forum where his son was due to assume the *toga virilis* (toga of manhood), a ceremony which marked his rite of passage to adulthood. Afterwards they made their way to the portico of Pompey adjoining the *curia* (fig. 8), expecting Caesar to arrive immediately since meetings of the senate traditionally began at dawn. Brutus and the other magistrates took their seats and began hearing petitions. As we noted in the previous chapter, a gladiatorial display, sponsored by Decimus Brutus, was due to be staged in the theatre of Pompey later in the day and it would serve as a useful distraction while the crime was being committed.

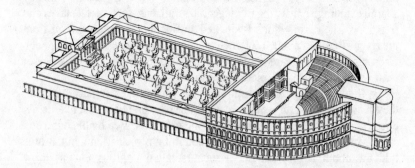

Fig. 8 Theatre and portico of Pompey. The *curia* is the square building on the left.

10 a.m.

At Caesar's house, however, all was not well. It is claimed that both he and Calpurnia had prophetic dreams: Caesar allegedly that he was borne aloft, clasping the hand of Jupiter; Calpurnia that she was cradling her bleeding husband in her arms. Caesar's dream anticipates his deification, whereas that of Calpurnia's anticipates the manner of his death. Both, therefore, are likely to have been invented to justify what subsequently happened. Even so, it is entirely plausible that the pair had a disturbed night and that for one reason or another they woke up in an anxious frame of mind.

As was customary after a disturbing dream, Caesar ordered the *haruspices*, experts in the Etruscan art of prophecy, to examine the entrails of the sacrificial victims to determine the will of the gods. Since they proved unfavourable, Caesar, yielding to pleas from Calpurnia, was on the point of sending Mark Antony to announce that he would not attend the senate when Decimus Brutus arrived. Hearing the cause of the delay, Decimus made light of Calpurnia's objections and pleaded earnestly with Caesar not to disappoint the senate. We need not believe Plutarch's allegation (*JC* 64) that Decimus told Caesar that it was proposing to give him the title of king outside Italy. All he needed to do was to point out that his absence would be taken as a further insult by an already aggrieved senate.

11 a.m.

Caesar departed from the *domus publica* around the fifth hour of the day; that is to say, between ten and eleven a.m. As soon as he emerged from his residence, a throng of petitioners, all eager to gain his attention, surrounded him. He was conveyed to the *curia* of Pompey in a litter, accompanied by a large entourage consisting of magistrates, citizens, foreigners, slaves and freedmen. The *curia*, which is situated outside the city walls not far from the river Tiber, lies about 1200 metres west of the *domus publica*. Though Caesar's way was cleared before him by *lictors*, it probably took him at least half-an-hour to complete the journey.

By late morning the conspirators had become extremely agitated; they feared that Caesar's delay meant their plan had been discovered. At one point during their long wait someone grasped Casca by the hand and said, 'you kept the secret from me although I am your friend, but Brutus told me about it'. At another a senator called Popilius Laenas drew Brutus and Cassius aside and said that he was 'praying for a favourable outcome to their plans'. To make matters worse, a slave of Brutus arrived with the news that his wife Porcia had died. It later turned out that she had only fainted; she had probably worked herself up into a frenzy of anxiety. Eventually the decision was taken to cancel the meeting and Caesar's golden curule chair was removed from the *curia*.

12 a.m.

Shortly afterwards Caesar arrived. As he was ascending the steps to the *curia*, he was handed a roll revealing the plot. Whether or not he suspected its contents, he left it unread. At the same time Popilius Laenas engaged him in animated conversation. The conspirators became so frightened by this that they signalled to one another that they would take their own lives rather than be apprehended. However, once they realised that Laenas was merely petitioning Caesar about a private matter, they recovered their spirits. When the auspices were taken, as was customary before any public meeting, it was reputedly discovered that one of the victims lacked a heart. Since this is a biological impossibility, we should probably take this to mean that the organs were extremely unhealthy. Though other sacrifices were performed with a similarly unpropitious outcome, Caesar decided to enter the *curia*.

Catching sight of the soothsayer Spurinna who had warned him to beware of the ides of March, Caesar jokingly accused him of being an impostor. Spurinna replied, 'the ides have indeed come but they have not yet gone'. It is interesting that Spurinna turns up again in the narrative. He is, of course, needed for dramatic closure, both to witness the fulfilment of his prophecy and to highlight the fact that the climactic moment has arrived. He also points up Caesar's scorn for religious observance and his disdain for any measures of self-protection.

Since it was a very important meeting, the *curia* is likely to have been packed. Many of those present were Caesar's recent nominees, perhaps taking their places in the senate for the first time. On the agenda were Mark Antony's objections to Caesar's nomination of P. Cornelius Dolabella, who was designated to replace him as suffect consul for the rest of the year. As Caesar passed inside the chamber, C. Trebonius, who was standing at the door, stepped forward and engaged Antony in conversation to prevent him from passing inside.[18]

Once the lustration had been performed and the meeting had been declared open, several conspirators rose from their benches and gathered around Caesar, who remained seated. Tillius Cimber began pleading with him to allow his brother to return from exile. This enabled Cimber to make physical contact with Caesar under the guise of supplication; and since the dictator could be guaranteed to reject his request, it added further evidence of the victim's autocratic bent.

When Caesar replied that Cimber was out of order, the latter grasped his purple toga to restrict his freedom of movement. Caesar cried out, 'this is violence!', whereupon Cimber exclaimed, 'What are you waiting for, friends?'. One of the two brothers named Casca tried to stab Caesar in the neck but missed and wounded him in the chest. Caesar now exclaimed, 'vile Casca!'. Managing to wrestle free of Cimber and grasping Casca's hand, he stabbed it with the *stylus* (writing implement) that he was holding. Then he sprang from his chair. While he was dragging Casca about, another conspirator stabbed him in the side. Cassius wounded him in the face, M. Brutus struck him in the thigh, and an otherwise unknown Bucolianus smote him in the back. As Brutus struck, he shouted the name of Cicero and congratulated him on the restoration of freedom (Cicero *Philippics* 2.28). From that point the victim ceased to put up further resistance. Since the doors of the *curia* were traditionally left open while the senate was in session, Antony must have heard Caesar's cries, which means that Trebonius had to use considerable force to restrain him. He may well have been selected for this task because of his size.

Both Suetonius and Cassius Dio report the tradition that Caesar's dying words were, 'you, too, child?', which he delivered in Greek. As members of Rome's intellectual élite, Brutus and Caesar would have been proficient in the language and doubtless conversed in it from time to time. Caesar's choice of Greek should therefore be construed as evidence of their intimacy. The word 'child' was also suggestive, for it implied that the crime was in essence one of parricide.[19]

Caesar fell beside the statue of Pompey. As he went down, he drew his toga over his head and covered his feet so that his last moments should not be witnessed. The conspirators continued hacking at his prostrate body, wounding him twenty-three times (or thirty-five times, if we are to believe Nicolaus of Damascus). Plutarch (*JC* 66.6) vividly reports that 'they all had to participate in the sacrifice and get a taste of the murder'. In the event this probably proved impractical. Though all the conspirators would have seen military action, they were not professional killers and may well have been extremely nervous. This is suggested by the report that they slid on Caesar's blood and injured one another in the scuffle.

Once they had desisted from the killing, Brutus stepped forward, intending to justify their crime to the senate. Before he could do so, however, the senators had fled, including Mark Antony, who escaped disguised in a plain brown tunic as worn by plebeians and barricaded himself in his house. Once news of the murder broke, panic spread throughout the city. The markets were ransacked and people locked themselves indoors, preparing to defend themselves from their roofs. Appian (*CW* 2.118) claims that many other people were killed that day, including some senators. The assassins conducted a lacklustre victory parade, waving their daggers in the air and calling upon the citizenry to embrace liberty. They took the precaution of wrapping their togas around their left arms to serve as shields in case of attack. A few senators, innocent of the crime, joined their ranks and claimed complicity in the murder. They later paid for their bravado with their lives. Lepidus, who happened to be in the forum when he learned of the murder, ran to the island in the river Tiber, where he had a legion of soldiers under his command. He hastily dispatched them to the Campus Martius and awaited orders from Antony.

3 p.m.

Caesar's body lay on the floor of the *curia* for some time until three slaves arrived and bore it back to the *domus publica* in a litter 'with one arm hanging out' – an affecting detail reported by Suetonius (*JC* 82). According to the physician Antistius, who performed a *post mortem*, none of the wounds was lethal 'except for the second one which the victim received in his breast'. His report indicates that the murder was a botched business, perpetrated by rank amateurs. Interestingly we do not know which of the conspirators delivered the second blow.

There is no knowing how long it took Caesar to die. Appian (*CW* 2.116) claims that a Greek friend of Caesar's named Artemidorus found the victim still breathing when he arrived at the *curia*. If the second wound hit an artery in the neck, death would have been swift and relatively painless; if not, it may well have been protracted and painful – all the more so in view of the twenty-two flesh wounds.

Antistius has the distinction of being the first physician in history to pronounce upon cause of death in the case of a violent killing. It is not clear why he was summoned nor on whose orders, though the finger of suspicion overwhelmingly points at Mark Antony. A cynic might argue that he co-opted the services of a physician partly to reveal the ignominy and incompetence of the crime, and partly to increase sympathy for the victim.

The conspirators' original plan had been to bear the corpse the short distance from the *curia* to the Tiber and then toss it unceremoniously into the water. However, they changed their minds for fear of antagonising the populace. This was a second blunder.

5 p.m.

The assassins, or 'liberators' as they liked to call themselves, took refuge on the Capitol, attended by Decimus Brutus' gladiators. When it became apparent that no more violence was planned, a number of sympathisers cautiously ascended the hill. Plutarch tells us that M. Brutus delivered a speech 'that was designed to win over the people and be appropriate to the occasion' (*Brutus* 18.10). This hardly amounts to a ringing endorsement of his oratorical performance. It is evident that the assassins had no coherent idea about how to 'liberate' Rome other than by slaying the tyrant. One and all they now displayed woeful political ineptitude. What should or would happen seems not to have crossed their minds.

6 p.m.

Later Brutus and Cassius descended from the Capitol into the forum. A number of eminent citizens conducted Brutus onto the rostra, where he delivered another speech justifying their deed. However, when the praetor Cornelius Cinna joined him and began to denounce Caesar, voices were raised in dissent. Brutus and Cassius again withdrew to the Capitol. According to Appian (*CW* 2.123), they sent messengers to Antony and Lepidus asking if their deed could be 'tolerated out of pity for the perpetrators and out of compassion for the city worn out by continuous civil war'. Antony's response was polite and non-committal.

11 p.m.

Antony now acted quickly. He obtained Caesar's private papers from his widow Calpurnia. These were to prove extremely useful, since, as we shall see, they would enable him to 'interpret' Caesar's final wishes as he saw fit and to appoint magistrates of his own choice. He also got his hands on Caesar's fortune, which probably amounted to about 100 million sesterces. The money was stored in the *domus publica* – evidently Caesar did not believe in banks. At the request of L. Calpurnius Piso the Vestal virgins handed over Caesar's will. Prior knowledge of its contents would give Antony a further advantage over the assassins, which he would use to devastating effect at the funeral.

* * * * *

Caesar's murder did not come as thunder out of a blue sky, as the poet Horace might have put it. On the contrary, the writing had been on the wall for some time. This leaves us with an endlessly fascinating question. It seems inconceivable that the victim was wholly unaware of the plot against his life, given the fact that he probably had a network of freedmen, clients and slaves gathering information on his behalf. If this is true, his observation the night before his murder that the best death is the one that comes unexpectedly takes on a peculiarly poignant significance. His dismissal of his Spanish bodyguard seems, moreover, to have been an act of reckless self-endangerment. Nor did it require much intelligence to deduce that his final public appearance was a moment of high risk.

One conclusion is that Caesar saw his death coming and walked calmly towards it, preferring, in his own words, to die once than a thousand times.[20] An alternative interpretation is that Caesar had lived so long with the threat of danger hanging over his head that he had almost come to believe that he was immortal. Ever since his election as *pontifex maximus* eighteen years before, he had had to reckon with the possibility of assassination and, as the reports of four previous plots against his life make clear, that threat had in no way abated as his political stature had grown. It was the price he had to pay for occupying the limelight. Dio Cassius (*RH* 44.18.4) goes so far as to claim that Caesar entered the senate in an upbeat mood. It is possible that he was aware, either in general or in specific terms, of a plot against his life and that he simply scorned it, having long since learned to subdue fear. This attitude had stood him in good stead on the battlefield, where he had consistently taken unreasonable risks that had invariably paid off. To put it bluntly, did he or did he not realise that his luck had finally run out?

Caesar was exactly the same age as Rome's legendary founder Romulus when he was murdered, though we may plausibly suspect that Romulus' age was adjusted to correspond to his. The story of Romulus' dismemberment at the hands of a crowd of senators, as reported by Livy (1.16.4), is likely to be another *post eventum* invention to add further colour to the comparison.

The alleged omens that heralded his death demonstrate two important facts that the sources are eager to relay: first, that the victim had stirred up so much hatred that his death was indeed 'fated' in the sense that there were compelling reasons why a large number of senators would have wanted him dead; second, that he presumptuously chose to ignore all the warnings from the gods. Though these two 'facts' may seem at first sight to cancel each other out, the Roman mind would have judged them to be complementary. Briefly put, Caesar died, and deserved to die, because he was the kind of person who disdained the warnings which the gods had scattered across his path. Somewhat later this interpretation may have been modified by the Caesarian faction to suggest that his death had, in a more neutral sense, been 'fated'.

We do not know how many of the omens were invented *post eventum*. With the exception of the inauspicious sacrifice performed outside the senate, which may well be historical, there is every reason to believe that most were fabricated after his death. It is highly likely that the dream attributed to Caesar of clasping Jupiter by the hand was intended to justify his deification. The other omens may be the product of the anti-Caesarian propaganda disseminated after his death to palliate the enormity of the crime. The narrative of the murder itself, however, is on *a priori* grounds likely to have been preserved and embellished by pro-Caesarian sympathisers, whose object was to exaggerate the vulnerability of the victim on the one hand, and the cowardice and callousness of his assassins on the other.

Chapter 10

The Funeral

At the senate meeting held on 17th March Ti. Claudius Nero, father of the future emperor Tiberius and currently married to Livia (later wife of the emperor Augustus), chose to ignore the fact that the 'liberators', as Brutus *et al.* now styled themselves, had violated their sacred oath by · taking the life of a man they had sworn to protect and recommended that they receive special honours. Such a gesture would not have been without precedent, since the Athenians had officially granted heroic status to Harmodius and Aristogeiton for slaying the tyrant Hipparchus at the end of the sixth century – a fact of which all educated Romans could be expected to be aware.

Antony blocked Nero's proposal by shrewdly pointing out that, if Caesar were to be dubbed a tyrant, all his decrees, including those nominating many of the assassins to magistracies, would automatically be rendered invalid. So instead the senate agreed to declare an amnesty and acknowledged simply that Caesar had been slain by 'honourable and patriotic citizens'. Antony also proposed that Caesar's unpublished projects should have the force of law. This, too, was passed. It put Antony in a very favourable position, since, with exclusive access to Caesar's papers, he was now in a position to fabricate whatever he wanted.

Either on this occasion or possibly a day or two later the senate discussed arrangements for Caesar's burial. Antony proposed that his will should be read out at the funeral and the body exposed to public view with all due honours. This was opposed by Cassius but agreed to by Brutus and duly ratified – another tactical error on Brutus' part which was to prove fatal to the assassins' hopes. Though it was still early days, public opinion had not rallied behind them to the degree they had hoped. When the praetor Cornelius Cinna arrived at the senate, he was stoned and forced to flee because on the previous day he had disdainfully removed his praetorial robe and trampled it in the dust, declaring that he would not accept 'the gift of a tyrant'. An irate mob pursued him to his house and was on the point of setting it on fire when Lepidus and his soldiers arrived to restore order. After the senate had dispersed, Antony sent his two-year old son to the Capitol as a hostage and invited Cassius home to dinner. Brutus for his part went home with Lepidus.

Caesar's funeral probably took place on 20th March. The general arrangements had been established long ago. Caesar had expressed his wish to be buried in the tomb of the Julii in the Campus Martius, beside the ashes of his beloved daughter Julia.[21] Probably as well he had requested a *funus publicum* (public funeral). This at any rate is what his father-in-law L. Calpurnius Piso now demanded. Public funerals, to which all citizens were invited, were accorded exclusively to benefactors of the Republic. They were organised by the magistrates and paid for by the state.

The corpse was washed and anointed by women and then displayed in the *domus publica*. In the case of a public funeral the lying in state might last as long as seven days but on this occasion the custom was severely curtailed, due to the condition of the corpse. Possibly only Caesar's immediate family were permitted to view it.

The senate was wholly unprepared for the outpouring of popular sentiment that Caesar's funeral unleashed. The only comparable event in living memory was Sulla's funeral, also held at public expense, which had taken place a generation earlier, but the scenes of grief on that occasion must have paled by comparison with those to which Caesar's obsequies gave rise.[22] Rome's population at this time was about three-quarters of a million; we can well imagine that few would have stayed at home. Whatever the size of the forces of public order, they were quickly overwhelmed by the spontaneous outburst of sympathy for the victim and, as so often happens, one act of violence generated random criminality on a vast scale, till the whole city erupted.

The cortège travelled from the *domus publica* to the rostra, a distance of only about 110 metres. Torches and tapers were borne in procession. Most Roman funerals were held at night and the custom of bearing torches was adhered to even when a funeral took place in daylight. Musicians, dancers and mime artists who acted out short scenes (possibly drawn from Caesar's life), as well as Caesar's many clients or dependents, preceded the casket. Hundreds of his ex-slaves, all emancipated by the terms of his will, also participated. Wax *imagines* or effigies of the deceased's ancestors were borne in the procession. This was a mark of distinction, since the right of keeping *imagines* was restricted to members of the nobility. *Lictors* also preceded the casket, bearing their *fasces* upside down as a sign of mourning. There is no agreement in our sources as to whether the casket was open or closed: though it was Roman practice to leave it open, on this occasion it may well have been closed, since Caesar had probably received a number of face wounds.

Behind the casket came a long line of senators, magistrates and foreign dignitaries, who wished to bestow their respect and sympathy. Cleopatra was not among them. A gilded shrine had been set up on the rostra, replicating in miniature the temple of Venus Genetrix that Caesar had erected in the Julian Forum. Inside was an ebony couch with gold and purple coverlets, on which the casket was laid. A 'trophy', similar to the kind of monument that was erected on the battlefield following a military victory, was set up at the head of the couch. It was draped in the bloodied toga that Caesar had been wearing on the day of his death as a graphic reminder of his violent end.

The ceremony began with the recitation of extracts from a selection of Roman tragedies that were intended to induce pity for the victim. A series of gladiatorial combats took place (fig. 4, p. 28), no doubt reminiscent of those that Caesar had held on behalf of his father and aunt. Their purpose was to appease the angry spirit of the murdered dead. We do not know precisely when in the whole proceedings Antony read out Caesar's will but it was this action which caused the tide of sympathy to turn irreversibly against the assassins. As Plutarch (*Brutus* 20) observes, 'when it was revealed that Caesar had left 75 drachmas (i.e. *denarii*)[23] to every single Roman citizen and had bequeathed his gardens on the far side of the Tiber, where there is now a temple of Fortune, to the citizenry, an incredible feeling of goodwill and love seized hold of the people'. Likewise Appian (*CW* 2.143) writes: 'there were wailing and dirges for a very long time, and the armed men beat upon their shields, and gradually people began to change their mind about the amnesty'. And well they might.

We shall never know whether Antony anticipated and intended the uproar that greeted the reading of the will but it is entirely possible that the public response vastly exceeded his expectations. His eulogy is not preserved, though Suetonius (*DJ* 84) claims that it was brief. This is confirmed by Cicero who, though not present, probably read a published version. He quoted the expressions 'a very great man' and 'a most distinguished citizen' in his correspondence; and he later maintained that it was Antony's speech that inflamed the populace.

When Antony revealed Caesar's body, gutted with wounds, matters got completely out of control. The centurions standing on the rostra revolved a wax image of the deceased by means of a mechanical device so as to exhibit its wounds from every angle. A group of mourners broke through the cordon of legionaries, ascended the rostra, removed the corpse from its shrine, and raised it onto their shoulders – an exceptional honour. A violent argument now broke out as to where Caesar should be cremated. Some suggested carrying his corpse up onto the Capitol so that a cult could be established in his honour inside the temple of Capitoline Jupiter, though its priesthood managed to deter them. Meanwhile another group began constructing a pyre in front of the *regia*, using benches and chairs and whatever else was available. Soldiers donated their arms, entertainers threw in their robes, and the general public contributed jewellery and clothing.

As soon as the funeral was over, mob violence broke out. One gang, seizing firebrands from the pyre, headed off to the houses of Brutus and Cassius intending to burn them down. Being prevented by the neighbours, they vented their anger on a certain C. Helvius Cinna, a poet, whom they mistook for Cornelius Cinna, the praetor who had spoken critically about Caesar. Appian chillingly reports that the mob tore him to pieces like wild beasts 'so that no part of him was found for burial'. The victim of mistaken identity was actually a supporter of Caesar and an accomplished poet, the author of a homoerotic poem in a new literary genre. His death at the hands of a lynch mob so alarmed Brutus and Cassius that they fled from Rome, either on the night of the funeral or a few days later.

The pyre burned for several days. Foreigners, especially Rome's Jewish population, were especially demonstrative in their grief and visited the site several nights in a row. They had been ardent supporters of Caesar during the Civil War because Pompey had defiled their holy of holies in Jerusalem (see p. 50). Caesar, in recognition of their help during his Egyptian campaign, had excluded them from his blanket ban on religious associations and permitted them to build a synagogue in Rome.

When the pyre was eventually extinguished on Antony's orders, Caesar's ashes, to the degree that they could be separated from the rest of the burnt material, were collected by his freedmen and spirited away for burial. Probably they were interred in the Campus Martius beside those of his daughter Julia, as originally intended. Later Augustus removed Pompey's statue and walled up the *curia*, renaming the ides of March Parricide Day (Suetonius *DJ* 88, *Divus Augustus*, 31.5). This was in acknowledgement of the fact that Caesar had been declared *parens patriae* (father of the fatherland). No meeting of the senate could ever be convened on that day again. Later still the *curia* was converted into a public latrine (Cassius *RH* 47.19.1).

As Appian (*CW* 2.148) reports, an unofficial cult was instituted over the spot where the cremation had taken place.[24] A certain Herophilus (or Amatus, according to other sources), claiming to be the grandson of C. Marius, sought without success to stir up trouble and was executed for his pains. Subsequently some of Caesar's supporters built an altar and a marble column in the forum.

Once Caesar had been officially deified (see p. 91) work began on a temple to the 'divine' Julius. It was interrupted by the civil war that followed (p. 92). The eventual dedication of the temple by Augustus on 18th August 29 BCE was celebrated with magnificent games. Inside it stood a colossal statue of Caesar, holding the staff of an augur. He would be worshipped in the heart of the forum for centuries to come. The temple was repaired by the emperor Hadrian in the early second century CE and survived into late antiquity. In the sixteenth century, however, it served as a quarry for the papal building programme. The entire superstructure has disappeared and only the infill of the podium survives.

The custom of placing flowers at the feet of the statue of Julius Caesar. in Via dell' Impero in Rome annually on the ides of March, which was introduced by Mussolini, is observed to this day.

Chapter 11

The Avenger

The assassins had been completely outmanoeuvred. They had naively believed that, once they had rid Rome of its hated tyrant, the ship of state would right itself and they would be hailed as 'liberators'. They had not allowed for the dangerous power vacuum that Caesar's murder produced. In the weeks that immediately followed we learn little about their movements. Decimus Brutus and C. Trebonius took up their governorships in Cisalpine Gaul and Asia respectively. The rest presumably remained on their estates in the country. When Marcus Brutus asked his cousin what he thought they should do, the latter suggested that they should 'bow to the dictates of fortune' (Cicero *Letters to Friends* 11.1.3). Since they had no legions under their command, there was in fact little they could do. One is therefore forced to agree with Cicero's verdict: 'the deed was done with manly courage but childish policy' (*Letters to Atticus* 15.4).

Much of what followed over the next two-and-a-half years depended on the fickle wind of public opinion, which was constantly being directed by subtle and not so subtle forms of propaganda. At the outset the political situation was extremely unstable. There were three main groupings: the supporters of the assassins, including Cicero; the Caesarians, led by Mark Antony and several of the tribunes of the *plebs*; and the moderates, who were eager to avoid yet another bout of civil war.

The unexpected fly in the ointment was Caesar's heir, the eighteen-year-old C. Octavius (pl. vii), whose character and determination were completely underestimated, not least by Cicero, who referred to him disparagingly as an *adulescentulus,* a 'mere stripling' (*Letters to Brutus* 26.3). When news reached him at Apollonia of his grand-uncle's death, he hastily returned to Italy where he was greeted enthusiastically by Caesar's veterans as soon as he stepped on shore at Brundisium. He must have realised there and then that he could count on their unwavering support should he decide upon a military undertaking. Rejecting the advice of his mother, Atia, and stepfather, L. Philippus, who recommended that he opt for a quiet life, as well as that of Cicero, a family friend who was roped in to lend extra weight to their arguments, Octavius decided to accept Caesar's inheritance. He arrived in Rome in April and was formally adopted as C. Julius Caesar Octavianus.[25] Modern historians generally refer to him as Octavian, until his assumption of the title 'Augustus' in 27.

The place where Caesar's body had been cremated in the forum quickly became a focus for the grief that his death continued to provoke. In April Antony's consular colleague P. Cornelius Dolabella removed the temporary altar. Cicero, still optimistic that the assassination would eventually win general acceptance, took this to be a propitious sign that a wind of change was in the air. He therefore wrote to Atticus (*Letters to Atticus* 14.16.2) saying that it looked as if Brutus 'could now walk through the forum wearing a golden crown'. Even so, he was growing increasingly frustrated by Brutus' want of initiative. In early May he wrote again to Atticus saying that if Brutus did not attend the senate meeting on 1st June, he had little prospect of retaining popular support.

. At the end of May Brutus and Cassius wrote to Antony from their country estates, explaining that they wanted to come to Rome but were fearful of their reception by Caesar's veterans. They were eager, they said, to discover Antony's intentions. Their letter was in effect a frank admission of political weakness and, whatever response it elicited, they decided to stay put. Meanwhile, when Octavian presented himself before Antony, the latter behaved towards him with barely disguised hostility, denying him access to Caesar's fortune.

Antony had originally been given Macedonia as his province. At the meeting of the senate on 1st June he managed to exchange it for Cisalpine and Transalpine Gaul, and to extend his command for five years. This was, of course, Caesar's old province and his request, duly granted, must have aroused deep suspicions as to his intentions. A few days later, again on Antony's prompting, the senate made Brutus and Cassius a derisory offer of the corn-commissionerships in the provinces of Asia and Sicily. It was a calculated insult. Brutus and Cassius met at Antium (modern Anzio) to discuss the situation. When Cassius angrily declared that he had no intention of accepting, Brutus' mother Servilia undertook to see to it that the senatorial resolution was rescinded (Cicero *Letters to Atticus* 15.11).

As we have already seen in Caesar's early bid for popular recognition during his aedileship, one of the most effective ways of gaining public support in Rome was by hosting lavish games. In his capacity as urban praetor, M. Brutus now sought to recover the goodwill of the *plebs* by staging the Apollinarian games (held in honour of Apollo), which were

Plate vii.   Octavian

 [a] Brutus (obverse)

b] Cap of liberty and
daggers (reverse)

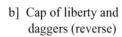 [c] Pompey

Plate viii.

scheduled for 6th-13th July. Still fearful of his reception in the capital he did not preside in person.

Whatever goodwill accrued to him from this spectacle was, immediately cancelled out by the games in honour of Venus Genetrix, which Octavian hosted a few days later on 20th July. These matched, if they did not outdo, those staged by Brutus. In fact, they may have taken the form of funeral games in Caesar's honour; the practice of holding funeral games for mighty warriors had a very long ancestry in the ancient world. In the *Iliad* Homer provides a lengthy description of those staged on behalf of Patroklos by Achilles. If indeed these games were intended in part to honour Caesar, we have early evidence of Octavian's genius for using propaganda to promote his political agenda.

What rendered this event all the more remarkable was the appearance of a comet in the early evening sky, just when the spectators were pouring out of the amphitheatre. Traditionally the appearance of a comet was viewed in antiquity as a harbinger of famine, plague, war or some similar catastrophe. On this occasion, however, as Octavian stated later in his lost autobiography, the *plebs* interpreted the comet as signifying 'that the *anima* or soul of Caesar had been received among the immortal gods' (Pliny *Natural History* 2.93). Catasterism (the belief that the dead are translated into stars) was almost certainly derived from the Greeks; Caesar's illustrious mythological precedents included the heavenly twins, Castor and Pollux.[26]

The comet certainly contributed to the belief in Caesar's apotheosis, though we do not know to what extent Octavian himself may have encouraged the interpretation. Only Servius, a fourth-century commentator on Vergil's *Aeneid*, suggests that he exploited it for his own purposes (6.790, 8.681). But even if Octavian did not do so initially, he quickly came to comprehend its potential value for his cause, since there is evidence to suggest that he attached a star to Caesar's statue in the forum shortly afterwards. In addition, coins were struck depicting Caesar's head with a star at his forehead. In 39 BCE Virgil, who by the time of his *Aeneid* had become 'propagandist' for the Augustan regime, published his earliest work the *Eclogues*, of which the fifth poem has two shepherds sing: one mourning the death of the apparently pastoral hero Daphnis, the other celebrating his apotheosis among the stars. Those critics who would read the poem allegorically see specific reference to the death and deification of Caesar and to the comet's appearance. Plutarch (*JC* 69) also mentions that the sun cast a pale and ineffective light throughout the year.

Towards the end of July the senate voted Brutus and Cassius the provinces of Crete and Cyrene – evidently Servilia had been true to her word – and in August they left Italy. Instead of proceeding to their provinces they went to Macedonia and Syria respectively. On 2nd October Antony denounced Caesar's assassins in a popular assembly. He even went so far as to suggest that Octavian had been involved in the conspiracy. Shortly afterwards Cicero began to attack Antony in a series of vituperative speeches known as the *Philippics*. He jestingly named them after the speeches that the Athenian politician Demosthenes had delivered against Philip II of Macedon, the implication being that Antony, like Philip, was seeking to achieve domination by devious means.

Early in December Decimus Brutus announced his refusal to hand over the province of Cisalpine Gaul to his successor and Antony travelled north with three legions to oppose him (fig. 2, p. 12). He succeeded in forcing Decimus to withdraw from the towns he was occupying and began besieging him in a fortress colony known as Mutina (Modena). To consolidate his claim to be acting with pious regard for Caesar's memory, Antony began growing a beard as a sign of mourning. It was a highly effective instrument of propaganda, yet one which cleverly avoided the suggestion that he was conducting a vendetta against the assassins. He did not shave it off until Caesar's murder had been avenged at Philippi.

In January 43 the new consul Aulus Hirtius left Rome to relieve the siege at Mutina. Two months later his colleague C. Vibius Pansa followed at the head of four legions of recruits. Octavian, recently awarded senatorial status, also participated. On 15th April a bitter battle was fought at Forum Gallorum. Though Antony was defeated, Pansa was mortally wounded. A second battle took place a week later. Again Antony was defeated but this time Hirtius was killed. The deaths of Hirtius and Pansa left Octavian in command of nine legions. He was now in a position to dictate terms to the senate: he sent a delegation of 400 centurions and soldiers to demand the consulship. Initially the senate was reluctant to comply with his demands, naively believing that the young man could be browbeaten into submission. On 19th August Octavian, following the example of Sulla and Caesar, marched on Rome. He occupied the city without bloodshed and was elected consul for 42, along with his cousin Q. Pedius. His adoption was confirmed and he undertook to avenge his adoptive father's death.

Soon afterwards a court was set up and all Caesar's assassins were condemned *in absentia*. In addition, a sentence of outlawry that had been passed on Antony was rescinded. Octavian and Antony now buried the hatchet and began working together. On 27th November Octavian, Antony and Lepidus officially appointed themselves 'triumvirs for the re-establishment of the Republic'. They thereby assumed supreme authority in the state, though the constitution continued to function as before. To exact vengeance on the assassins and their supporters, the triumvirs immediately resorted to licensed thuggery, reviving the tradition of Sulla's proscriptions.

On 1st January 42 the senate consecrated Caesar as a god. This enabled Octavian to style himself *divi filius* ('son of god'). Brutus countered by striking a *denarius* on the reverse of which was a *pileus* (cap of liberty, of the kind given to freed slaves) placed between two daggers. Below the cap was the legend *EID. MAR.* (*'Eides Martiae'*, see pl. viii, a and b). The archaic spelling of 'ides' was intended to evoke Rome's glorious republican past and to suggest that the 'liberators' were restoring her ancient freedoms. The choice of a *pileus* was also highly symbolic, since slaves were commonly freed on the death of their master, just as the Romans had been 'freed' by the assassins. The obverse of the coin bore the head of Brutus.

Late in the year Octavian and Antony left M. Lepidus in charge of Italy and went east to do battle with Brutus and Cassius. The two armies, consisting of about twenty legions on each side, met at Philippi in Macedonia. In the first battle, which took place on 14th November, Cassius was routed and committed suicide, believing that Brutus was about to be defeated. About three weeks later a second engagement took place in which Brutus, realising that the cause was lost, also took his own life. We can only speculate what fate would have awaited Brutus and Cassius had they survived. Many of the enemy, including Horace, destined to become one of the greatest Augustan poets, surrendered and were pardoned. The others fled to Sextus Pompeius, who was raising an army of fugitive Pompeians in Spain. As a gesture of reconciliation Antony sent Servilia her son's ashes; his head was contemptuously tossed at the feet of Caesar's statue in the forum.

> Almost none of the assassins survived Caesar more than three years or died a natural death. All were condemned to death and perished in various ways, some through shipwreck, some in battle. A few committed suicide using the same dagger with which they had stabbed Caesar. [Suetonius *DJ* 89]

C. Trebonius was murdered on the orders of Dolabella shortly after his arrival in Asia to take up the position of governor. Decimus Brutus was deserted by his men and killed in flight. The tribune Pontius Aquila forfeited his life at Mutina. L. Minucius Basilus was murdered by one of his own slaves in 43. Cicero was killed by bounty hunters in the grounds of his villa at Formiae while trying to escape by sea. When she was shown his dismembered head and right hand, Antony's wife Fulvia angrily stuck her hairpin into the tongue that had so savagely denounced her husband in the *Philippics*. The head and the hand were later nailed to the rostra in the forum, common practice in the case of traitors. Tillius Cimber, like many others, died at Philippi.

Nothing further is heard of Calpurnia. Despite her husband's infidelities (and his offer to divorce her so that he could marry Pompey's daughter), she seems to have been a loving and complaisant wife. Her failure to persuade Caesar to stay at home on the ides of March argues a lack of assertiveness and her disappearance from our records comes as no surprise. Though Caesar left no provision for Calpurnia in his will, this should not be taken as a snub, since women only infrequently inherited from their husbands. Following Caesar's death she had to vacate the *domus publica*. Presumably she went to live with her father; Piso died shortly afterwards and his daughter's subsequent fate is unknown. Brutus' wife Porcia became mentally deranged and was put on suicide watch by her friends. Denied access to other means of taking her own life, she swallowed coals from a brazier and died in horrible agony. Cleopatra slipped out of Rome shortly after Caesar's death, destined to live – and love – another day.

Over the years Octavian adopted a number of measures to strengthen his position, while taking care to distance himself from the political legacy of his great-uncle, as it had become something of a liability. Following the enforced retirement of Lepidus in 36, relations between Octavian and the other triumvir, Mark Antony, became increasingly strained and Rome plunged into more self-slaughter. Antony allied himself with Cleopatra, and in so doing gave insult to his wife Octavia, Octavian's sister. Following the deaths of Antony and Cleopatra, Octavian ordered the killing of Ptolemy XV Caesar (Caesarion) who had recently come of age. Whether or not Caesarion was Caesar's natural issue, he was determined that there should be no other claimant to his adoptive father's title.

In 27 Octavian, henceforth styling himself Augustus, established what is generally referred to as the principate – rule by the *princeps* ('first citizen'). It was in effect a disguised monarchy, though he was careful to avoid any suggestion of *regnum* (kingship). At an unknown date he ordered the removal of Pompey's statue from the *curia*, which he set up opposite the entrance to the theatre, perhaps to ally himself to the republican cause that Pompey and his supporters had represented. The *curia* itself was formally declared a *locus sceleratus* (a 'place accursed') and walled up. Still later it was converted into a public latrine. Nothing remains of it today except for some blocks of tufa in the Largo Argentina that probably date from the period of its conversion. The once *locus sceleratus* is now a sanctuary for Rome's stray cats.

Augustus also suppressed Caesar's youthful compositions – we should dearly like to know what they contained that he found so offensive. He may have ordered the publication of Cicero's correspondence, in part to reveal the hypocrisy of his dealings with Caesar. In 2 BCE he inaugurated a temple in honour of Mars Ultor ('avenger') in fulfilment of a vow that he had made before the battle of Philippi. Architecturally the temple resembled that of Venus Genetrix in the Julian Forum; in scale it was one and a half times larger than its predecessor.

Chapter 12

The Legacy

Caesar's most obvious bequest to the world is the Julian calendar. The earliest Roman calendar, which perhaps dated to the foundation of Rome in 753, consisted of ten lunar months from Martius (named after Mars, the god of war, because it signalled the beginning of the campaigning season) to December, the tenth month (Latin: *decimus*). The Romans had a ten-month calendar because they originally excluded the winter season from their reckoning. According to tradition, Januarius and Februarius were added in *ca* 700 BCE by Numa Pompilius, the second king of Rome. This meant that the civic calendar now consisted of 355 days. In an attempt to overcome the discrepancy between the solar and the civic year, the Romans occasionally intercalated (i.e. inserted) an extra month called Mercedonius, which was twenty-seven days in length. They also shortened Februarius to twenty-three (or twenty-four) days. The decision in any given year to intercalate rested with the priesthood and was probably somewhat arbitrary. Since magistracies were of one year's duration, we may assume that the priesthood sometimes intercalated for no better reason than to extend the period of office of a magistrate whom they favoured or were compelled to favour.

By 46 the civic calendar had fallen so far out of step with the solar calendar that no fewer than eighty days had to be intercalated. It was Caesar, who, in his capacity as supreme pontiff, took the radical step of aligning the calendar with the solar year and inserting an extra day every four years between 23rd and 24th Februarius. Plutarch (*JC* 59) claims that he took a leading role in the process, not only by studying the problem scientifically himself but also by making the correct calculation in consultation with leading mathematicians and astronomers. Whatever his contribution, he deserves full credit for having the vision to comprehend the benefits of a cycle that exhibited both precision and uniformity. He also determined that each month, except for Februarius, should be either thirty or thirty-one days in length. As we have seen, in February 45 the senate voted to re-name Quinctilis, the 'fifth' (*quintus*) month of the year, Julius (July) in his honour. Twenty years later, it would re-name Sextilis, the 'sixth' (*sextus*) month of the year in Augustus' honour.

With minor modifications the Julian calendar has remained in use to the present day. Little change was made until the sixteenth century when it became evident that the solar year was lagging eleven days behind the calendar year. This was a particular problem of the Church, since it meant that Easter was constantly moving further from New Year's Day. In 1583 Pope Gregory XIII decreed that 4th October should be followed by 15th October. The new calendar was called Gregorian.

France and Belgium and, more indirectly, Germany owe their identity as nations to Caesar, since the Rhine, which came to mark the northern limit of the Roman Empire, was not an ethnic boundary. In addition, Caesar's conquest meant that the empire was no longer focused exclusively on the Mediterranean. At the same time his proconsulship had dire consequences for the region. The requisitioning of food and supplies for his legions, combined with the disastrous effects of a prolonged war, made more devastating by punitive action on Caesar's part, brought about what Ernst Badian (1996, 781) has described as a 'human, economic, and ecological disaster probably unequalled until the conquest of the Americas'. Though Caesar's invasion of Britain was an abortive affair which had no military consequences whatever, his is the first recorded name in the island's history.

Caesar's legislative programme was largely characterised by the removal of acknowledged abuses. He comprehended that the empire could best work if it spread its benefits among the entire population. He paved the way for the regular staging of gladiatorial contests in Rome itself and throughout her empire. They became an institution which the emperors exploited to buy the favour of the *plebs*. He is often charged with failing to come up with any solution to Rome's ills other than holding onto the reins of power himself. However, we can just as well argue that no one man could have eliminated at a single stroke the causes which, since the time of his uncle Marius, had fostered civil war. Moreover, even if Caesar realised that the only answer to these ills lay in the establishment of one-man rule, as he may well have done, he must also have comprehended that he was hardly the person to bring about that state of affairs, given both his quick-fire temperament and the deep hostility he had aroused. Even so, Caesar deserves credit for having facilitated the conditions under which a disguised monarchy could come into being. It is also a fact that the principate would not have taken the form it did, had not Octavian learnt the lessons of Caesar's failure.

Caesar's name is synonymous with absolute power and rulers from Roman times onwards have taken his name in order to borrow some of his reflected glory. Octavian's assumption of 'Caesar' signalled his adoption into the Caesarian family, and the precedent was followed by all the emperors of the Julio-Claudian dynasty that he established. Under the succeeding Flavian dynasty precedence was granted to the title 'Augustus' over that of 'Caesar'. Later still, when it became necessary to divide the duties of the emperor between a senior and junior partner, the senior partner took the title 'Augustus' and his heir presumptive that of 'Caesar'. 'Caesar' continued to be an imperial title in the Byzantine world. Later hereditary European monarchs appropriated Caesar's name to lend authority to their dynastic claims. Ivan III, known as 'the Great' (1462-1505), assumed the title 'Tsar' (or Czar) to signal his establishment of a monarchical autocracy which, though Muscovite in origin, sought to incorporate all Russia. Following the victory by the German states in the Franco-Prussian War in 1871, king William of Prussia assumed the title 'Kaiser' when he was proclaimed emperor of a newly unified German nation. It is also possible that 'Shah', the title of the former incumbent of the peacock throne of Iran, derives etymologically from 'Caesar'.

The memory of Caesar's achievements has remained in the bloodstream of European civilization from late antiquity to the present day. Plutarch's pairing of him with Alexander the Great in his *Parallel Lives* says much about his military reputation in the early second century CE. As a third-century papyrus from the city of Dura-Europus on the Euphrates indicates, Rome's legions were still celebrating the anniversary of his deification well into the Christian era. Suliman the Magnificent is said to have had Caesar's *Commentaries* translated into Arabic. Caesar was a familiar figure in the Middle Ages, partly because Lucan's *Civil War* (or *Pharsalia*) was regularly read in schools. His *Commentaries* were first published in Rome in 1469 and subsequently translated into many European languages. He was even numbered among the nine kings on French playing cards of the fifteenth and sixteenth centuries. He became the standard by which to measure the extremes of human existence. Henry V in Shakespeare's play of that name is described as 'Caesar's equal in starry fame'. As 'Imperial Caesar, dead and turned to clay...' in *Hamlet* he is exemplary of the transitory nature of human fortune. Italian Jews still name their sons 'Cesare', thereby perpetuating the memory of his pro-Jewish sentiments.

Leaders bent on domination have often sought to model themselves on Caesar's character and to emulate his accomplishments, to such an extent that 'Caesarist' came to be applied to one of imperialist inclinations (see p. 102). In 1500 Cesare Borgia celebrated a lavish triumph in which he drew comparison between himself and Caesar.

Napoleon Bonaparte, perhaps more than anyone who has ever lived, was in thrall to his personality and achievements. He mentions Caesar frequently in his writings and saw himself as the protector of the French nation in the same way that Caesar had been protector of the Roman world. At the end of his life, imprisoned on St. Helena, Napoleon dictated his *Précis of the Wars of Caesar* in which, from the vantage-point of experience, he assessed the merits and defects of Caesar's military campaigns. So close was the identification that the philosopher and poet Goethe declared that Napoleon's wars were necessary to make Caesar understood. The Emperor Napoleon III, who was equally desirous of a flattering comparison, wrote a two-volume *History of Julius Caesar* (1865-9) in which he likens his uncle's captivity to Caesar's murder: 'two popular causes overthrown by a league which disguised itself under the mask of liberty'.

The dictator Benito Mussolini, aptly dubbed 'a sawdust Caesar' by a contemporary reporter, was merely the latest instauration, his rise to power precipitated by a legendary event known as the March on Rome, whose symbolic significance was borrowed wholesale from Caesar's march on Rome. In October 1922 a loyal band of poorly armed militiamen descended on the capital from towns in the north of Italy, threatening to bring about a revolution. Mussolini, conspicuous by his absence from the venture, delayed his arrival – by express train from Milan – until its success was assured. He professed to be following in the footsteps of Caesar, who, like him, had extirpated a corrupt republic for the benefit of the common people. He was subsequently sworn in as Italy's youngest prime minister. Next month *il Duce*, as he had begun to style himself (in imitation of the Latin '*dux*' – leader) assumed dictatorial powers.[27]

Chapter 13

The Verdict

His own wish was to surpass [his opponents] in justice and fairness, just as he had striven to surpass them in action.

Caesar on Caesar [*Civil Wars* 1.32]

How should we assess Caesar's career and personality? The jury is out and will doubtless remain out for all time. As Cicero (*in defence of Marcellus* 29) prophetically observed, 'among those yet unborn there shall arise, as there has arisen among us, sharp division. Some shall laud your achievements to the skies, others shall miss something in them'. Cicero was himself highly ambivalent. In the midst of his vitriolic attack upon Mark Antony he wrote:

In Caesar there was genius, calculation, memory, letters, industry, thought, diligence. He had done in war things, however disastrous to the state, yet at least great. Having for many years aimed at a throne, he had achieved his goal by great labour and great dangers. He had wooed the ignorant masses by shows, buildings, hand-outs and banquets. He had bound his own followers to him by rewards and his adversaries by a demonstration of clemency. In brief, he had already brought to a free community – partly by fear, partly by endurance – a habit of servitude.

[*Second Philippic* 45.116]

The most sincere testimony of affection towards Caesar comes from a certain C. Mattius, who wrote to Cicero in August 44:

I'm fully aware of the fact that people have been rubbishing me behind my back since Caesar's death. They consider it a stain on my character that I grieve for the loss of a close friend and resent the death of a man I loved. They maintain that one's country should take precedence over one's friends – as if it was

99

a foregone conclusion that Caesar's death was beneficial to the
Republic. I'm incapable of such subtle argumentation myself.
I freely admit that I have not scaled such heights of abstract
reasoning. I didn't take Caesar's side in the Civil War but I
didn't abandon him either, even though his behaviour offended
me. When my close friend won, I didn't cash in on his victory
by demanding a promotion or some monetary reward as others
did with their grubby hands open, even though they had less
influence with him than I did.   [*Letters to Friends* 11.28]

   In the century and a half after his death Caesar was the focus of works
in a variety of literary genres. The most eccentric of these is Ovid's epic
entitled *Metamorphoses*, written shortly before the poet's banishment
in 8 CE, which uses Caesar's transformation into a 'flaming star' as the
climax to the entire poem. 'No achievement of [Caesar's] was greater
than that of becoming the father of our emperor', Ovid ambiguously
declares (15.750-51). Since Ovid is noted for his subversive attitude
towards Roman mores, particularly those that were being advocated at
the time by Augustus himself, we may suspect more than a pinch of irony
in his lauding of Caesar. The account of the Civil War by the historian
Livy has not survived but it was evidently so partisan to the republicans
that Augustus dubbed him a 'Pompeian'.
   Lucan's ten-book epic poem entitled *Civil War* begins with Caesar's
crossing of the Rubicon and ends with the death of Pompey. Initially neutral
to Caesar, from Book 3 onwards the poet depicts Caesar as a bloodthirsty
egomaniac who rejoices in the spectacle of mutilated corpses and denies
the right of burial to his enemies. As the personification of cosmic energy
at its most ferocious, he is the destructive force that has caused the death
of the body politic. Since Lucan was forced to commit suicide in 65 CE by
the emperor Nero, the later books have been interpreted as a lament for
the loss of political freedom which had been brought about by the Civil
War and which the Julio-Claudians had done nothing to restore.
   When Plutarch sought to pair Alexander the Great with a Roman of
comparable military genius, his choice, as we have seen, fell upon Caesar.
When Suetonius undertook to write his *Lives of the Caesars*, he began
with Julius Caesar, thereby emphasising his pivotal role as the divine
founder and eponym of the Julio-Claudian dynasty. The designation 'first
of the Caesars', which seems to have taken root only in the reign of the
emperor Trajan (98-117), was also instrumental in promoting the notion
that Caesar's career was a critical stepping-stone between the republican
and monarchical systems.

Caesar's character and achievement were a lively source of controversy in the Middle Ages. The scholastic philosopher and theologian Thomas Aquinas (*A Commentary on the Sentences of Peter Abelard* 2.44.2) argued that his murder was justified on the grounds that he had seized power by violent means. For some early Italian humanists, ill-educated in Roman history, Caesar exemplified the highest human values. Dante, who understood little of the political alignments in late republican Rome, was nonetheless engrossed by its personalities. In the *Inferno* he assigns Caesar an honoured place among virtuous pagans in the first circle of Hell, alongside such heroes as Hector and Aeneas (4.123). Somewhat paradoxically C. Scribonius Curio, the tribune who, acccording to Lucan (*CW* 1.273-91), prompted Caesar to cross the Rubicon when he was wavering, is cast into the ninth Bolgia for having 'drowned all Caesar's doubts'. 'His tongue cleft right to the gorge', Curio takes his place alongside other distinguished sowers of schism, including the prophet Mohamed (28.97-102). Brutus and Cassius meanwhile are cast into the deepest circle of Hell for betraying their benefactor and friend, to keep company with no less a turncoat than Judas Iscariot (34.64-69). Paradoxically again in *Purgatorio* Dante, imitating Lucan, selects Caesar's deadly enemy Cato, whom he identifies not as a suicide but as a martyr who laid down his life in the cause of liberty, to be the guardian of the path to spiritual freedom (1.31-108). Finally in *Paradiso* Caesar is assigned a place of honour alongside Justinian and Charlemagne, as the disseminator of peace throughout the Roman Empire and the manifestation of God's purposes on earth (6.57-66). Likewise for Coluccio Salutati, Chancellor of Florence, Caesar enjoyed the status of a pagan saint and was almost on an equal footing with Christ himself: 'Judas betrayed the God-man, and Cassius and Brutus treacherously slew Caesar, the image, as it were, of divinity in the rightfulness of his rule' (quoted in Baehr 1998, 32). The humanist poet and scholar Petrarch wrote a biography of the dictator, though when he undertook an epic on a Roman theme, he rejected Caesar as his model, regarding him as a tyrant and a man of loose morals; instead he chose Scipio Africanus, the vanquisher of Hannibal.

Caesar's ambivalence as a historical character made him an ideal subject for dramatic portrayal from the middle of the sixteenth century onwards, as we shall see in the next chapter. For Machiavelli, author of *The Prince* (1532), Brutus and Cassius were champions of liberty, whereas Caesar was 'the first tyrant in Rome' (*Discourses* 3.6). Michel de Montaigne, while speaking of 'the frenzied passion of Caesar's ambition', also saw in him 'the most richly endowed nature that ever appeared on earth' (*Essays* 2.33). As one of the first modern writers to appreciate Caesar's *Commentaries*, he also praised him for 'the purity and matchless polish of his language which surpassed that of all other historians' (*Essays* 2.10). John Milton, in his political treatise entitled *A Defence of the People of England* (ch. 5), which is effectively a defence of regicide, evinced a reluctant admiration, declaring, 'If ever any tyrant were to be spared, I would wish it to be he: for although he rushed a kingship upon the Republic somewhat too violently, yet he was perhaps most worthy of kingship'.

The philosopher and jurist Montesquieu, who, like Montaigne, frequently cited Caesar's life as an exemplum, declared in *The Spirit of the Laws* that 'Caesar's bloody toga reduced the Romans to their former servitude' (part 2, ch.15). He also congratulated him for preserving an appearance of equality while in effect ruling as a monarch (19.3). For Thomas de Quincey (*The Caesars*, ch. 1) he was 'the foremost man not only of his contemporaries, but also of men generally'. De Quincey picturesquely compared the destruction of the Roman Republic at his hands to the deflowering of a virgin, who in undergoing this act exchanged 'the imperfect and inchoate condition of a mere *femina* (woman) for the perfections of a *mulier* (wife)'. Byron, though he admired Caesar for his brilliant gifts, nonetheless concluded: 'And what have Caesar's deeds and Caesar's fame/Done for the earth? We feel them in our shame' (*The Island*, 1823). Goethe called Caesar's murder 'the most senseless deed in all of history' (quoted in Habicht, 1990, 131, n.30).

In the nineteenth century Caesar's career and personality became a focus of intense debate among political analysts, who discovered a modern analogy in the tensions between his style of leadership and his power base. Following the accession of Napoleon III as Emperor of France in 1852, the term 'Caesarism' was invented to describe a regime that combined authoritarianism with populism, which contemporary intellectuals identified as features shared in common by both the Second Empire and Caesar's dictatorship.[28] In Germany the debate took the form of yearning for a 'strong man' to achieve political unification. Georg Friedrich Hegel characterised Caesar as one of history's greatest achievers, whose personal goals were consistent with the demands of what he called the World-Spirit. Brutus and his co-conspirators by contrast were the victims of what he called a 'remarkable hallucination', which led them to believe that if Caesar were removed, the Republic would be restored.[29]

Adulation of Caesar became almost a trope among German historians. In *The History of Rome* (1856-85) Theodor Mommsen, following in Hegel's wake, described Caesar as the 'sole creative genius of Rome and the last produced by the ancient world'. Mommsen ended his history just before Caesar's death, evidently because he was incapable of bringing himself to describe his assassination. His lengthy eulogy concludes with the words: 'Caesar was the entire and perfect man'.[30] Jacob Burkhardt called Caesar 'perhaps the most gifted of mortals', compared with whom 'all others who are called great are one-sided'. A contrary note was struck by Eduard Meyer in his provocatively entitled *Caesar's Monarchy and Pompey's Principate* (3rd edn 1922). Meyer saw Caesar as a man devoid of any ideals and driven solely by personal ambition. Though he rejected the notion that Caesar sought to introduce a monarchy early on in his career, Meyer argued that in his final days he was manoeuvring to establish a divine monarchy on the Egyptian model and that it was for this reason that he permitted honours to be heaped upon him.

The German fascination with Caesar continued after the country's defeat in World War I, anticipating the advent of the Führer and outliving his demise. Friedrich Gundolf, who wrote a work translated as *The Mantle of Caesar* (1925), examined Caesar's reputation throughout history up until the time of Napoleon. He began somewhat chillingly, 'Today, as the need for a strong man is articulated…we wish to remind the over-eager of the great man to whom the highest authority owes its name and has for centuries owed its ideal: Caesar'. For Matthias Gelzer (1969 [1st edn 1921], 330f.) he was 'the greatest genius produced by Rome'. Christian Meier (1982, 484) wrote: 'The combination of brilliance – personal, not institutional brilliance – and power that we find in Caesar is probably almost unique in the whole of history'.

In the end, all judgments are partial and flawed. As Zvi Yavetz (1971, 191) remarked, 'The motley assortment of Caesars that has been presented in modern historiography illustrates the validity of the dictum that all history is contemporary history'. Perhaps more than anyone who ever lived Caesar embodied the principle of polarity. We are trapped between admiration of his vision and idealism on the one hand, however perverted the use to which he put these qualities, and condemnation of the havoc he caused on the other hand, albeit consequent, to a large degree, upon pre-existing evils. We admire Caesar for his unfettered and noble spirit; we deplore him for his scorn of constitutional propriety. He brought about the ruin of the Republic; he prepared the ground for a stable and lasting monarchy. He was the spiritual founder of fascism; he was the darling of the Roman *plebs*. He was an audacious military genius; he was a cynical and manipulative demagogue. Like Shakespeare's Brutus, we can state without fear of contradiction, 'Oh, Julius Caesar, though art mighty yet. Thy spirit walks abroad'.

Simply put, he extended the bounds of human possibility.

Chapter 14

The Media

Caesar's life and times have everything going for them in terms of romance, adventure, conspiracy, high stakes, intrigue and danger. It is hardly surprising that playwrights, composers, film producers and novelists have been inspired by this irresistible combination. Two episodes in particular, Caesar's dalliance with Cleopatra and his assassination, have repeatedly been reinterpreted in the media. The main sources are Plutarch's *Lives*, the pro-Caesarian *Commentary on the Alexandrine War*, and Lucan's *Civil War*, all of which were popular texts in the Renaissance. Plutarch serves as the model for treatments of Caesar's assassination, the *Commentary on the Alexandrian War* for the details of his sojourn in Egypt (though Cleopatra is conspicuously absent), while Lucan introduces the character of Pompey's grieving widow Cornelia, thereby further enhancing what executive producers today would call the 'feminine interest'.

1. Caesar on Stage

The earliest playwright to put Caesar on stage was Marc Antoine Muret, whose *Julius Caesar* (1553) was written in Latin in the style of a Greek tragedy, with a chorus of Roman citizens. Over the next hundred years several other Caesar plays were performed. They include Jacques Grévin's *César* (1561), Thomas Kyd's *Cornelia* (1594), an anonymous *Caesar's Revenge* (*ca.* 1595?), and George Chapman's *Caesar and Pompey* (*ca* 1613?).

The most celebrated is, of course, Shakespeare's *Julius Caesar*, first performed at the Globe Theatre in 1599 and the first of his Roman plays, which borrowed little from any of them. Shakespeare's main source was Plutarch's *Lives* in the translation by Sir Thomas North (1st edn. 1579; 2nd edn. 1595), in turn based on an earlier, French translation. Pierre Corneille's *The Death of Pompey* (1643), for which the principal source was Lucan, presents Caesar as a naked opportunist who capitalises upon the murder of Pompey to advance his ambition, while dispensing platitudinous courtesies to his widow Cornelia. In Voltaire's *The Death of Caesar* (1734), more melodrama than tragedy, Caesar takes on the role of a doting father who, shortly before his assassination, hands Brutus a letter from his mother Servilia revealing that he, Caesar, is Brutus' father – a somewhat desperate plot-contrivance designed to create in Brutus an intolerable conflict between his filial and his patriotic duty.

Shakespeare's *Julius Caesar*, which begins with the Lupercalia and ends at Philippi, explores the unfathomable nature of the truly great. His Caesar arouses fear and loathing among his peers but love and devotion among the rabble. Likewise his dignity and authority are contrasted with his vulnerability and frailty. He is deaf in his right ear (an invention of Shakespeare's) and experiences an epileptic seizure as the 'stinking breath' of the Roman mob assails his nostrils precisely when he is being offered the crown. He is preoccupied throughout with his image and refers to himself almost invariably in the third person, a device which Shakespeare borrows from the *Commentaries*. This distances Caesar not only from those around him but also from himself. A memorable example is his observation on the morning of the ides:

> Caesar should be a beast without a heart
> If he should stay at home today for fear.
> No, Caesar shall not. Danger knows full well
> That Caesar is more dangerous than he.
> [Act II Scene 2, 42-5]

Since Caesar is accompanied by an entourage, we never enter into his private world, as we do, through extended soliloquies like those of Cassius and Brutus. He makes only five appearances, three of which are under one minute in duration; and he is dead before the play is half-over. We are as much reliant upon the observations of others for our estimate of his personality as we are upon his own statements and actions. These observations in turn are often contradictory, as when Mark Antony in his funeral address repeatedly challenges Brutus' claim that Caesar was 'ambitious' (Act III Scene 2).

Of the many different interpretations which Shakespeare's play has received, there is space to mention only three. When *Julius Caesar* was first produced in the USA in 1770, shortly before the outbreak of the War of Independence, it was interpreted as an attack on autocracy, foreshadowing the colonies' war of emancipation against a brutal tyrant. 'The noble struggles for Liberty by that renowned patriot Marcus Brutus', the billing read. One-and-a-half centuries later, in the wake of the rise of the European dictatorships, Shakespeare's Caesar came to be regarded as an archetypal fascist. In 1937 Orson Welles directed a drastically slimmed-down version, subtitled *Death of a Dictator*, using pictures from the 1936 Nazi rally at Nürnburg as a backdrop to Mark Antony's funeral oration. Caesar (played by Joseph Holland) was depicted as the embodiment of totalitarianism with 'striding height, jutting chin, cross-belted military tunic, sleek modern breeches' (*Time Magazine* 22/11/1937). Welles' production laid the blame for the rise of fascism squarely at the feet of the masses so as to underscore the destructive power that dictators exert over their subjects. He achieved this in part by giving special emphasis to the scene where Cinna the poet is lynched by a violent mob seeking revenge for the death of Caesar. Also memorable was the Royal Shakespeare Company's 1972 production under the direction of Trevor Nunn. Nunn wanted to convey the impression that Caesar (played by a black leather-clad Mark Dignam) had in his own words reached 'a point of dangerous insanity'. Senators and the rabble clicked their heels and gave fascist salutes. The set was dominated by a sixteen-foot high statue which made palpable Cassius' description of Caesar as a Colossus, under whose huge legs 'petty men…walk and peep about'.

Shakespeare's portrait of Caesar has been frequently targeted by critics for its negativity. The essayist William Hazlitt wrote, 'We do not much admire the representation here given of Julius Caesar... he makes several vapouring and rather pedantic speeches, and does nothing'. Its most virulent critic, however, was G.B. Shaw, who described it as 'an admitted failure'. In *The Saturday Review* he complained at Shakespeare's 'travestying of a great man as a silly braggart'. In the preface to his *Caesar and Cleopatra*, which received its première in Chicago in 1901, he stated, no doubt in self-aggrandising mock rivalry, that he was making 'an offer of my Caesar to the public as an improvement upon Shakespeare's'. In the event, the two plays could hardly be more different. Shakespeare's is a double tragedy, Shaw's a light-hearted drawing-room comedy, in which Caesar instructs Cleopatra in the art of being a queen.

Shaw, whose portrait of Caesar was drawn from Theodor Mommsen's adulatory assessment in *History of Rome* (1856-85), invested his creation with all the classic Shavian virtues. As Michael Holroyd states in his biography, he is Shaw himself, 'a figure to promote his way of life and dramatize his philosophy'. That is to say, he is easy-going, witty, indifferent to his own welfare, forgiving of his enemies, lacking in malice, and tolerant of human weakness – a true representative, in other words, of the next stage of human evolution. He and the Egyptian Sphinx,

with whom he memorably compares himself, are 'strangers to the race
of men', though 'no strangers to each other'. At the same time Shaw's
Caesar manifests some endearing Shavian weaknesses. Most notably,
he is preoccupied with his waning sexual attractiveness, a facet of his
identity that is highlighted by Cleopatra's simpering flirtatiousness. But
though 'easily deceived by women', he exhibits the utmost propriety in
his relationship with the young queen (who is presented, incidentally, as
a young girl of sixteen, rather than as a woman of twenty-one). As Shaw
himself observed, 'the whole play would be revolting if Caesar were an old
man seducing a young girl'. Theirs then is a relationship that belongs more
to the Victorian nursery than to Clinton's west wing.

Though Cleopatra calls Caesar an 'old gentleman', he courageously
saves her by an Olympian swimming feat, thereby implicitly rebutting
the claim made by Shakespeare's Cassius that he all but drowned in the
Tiber when they swam in competition against one another. He is 'appalled
and disconcerted' when Pompey's head is brought to him, declaring
his dead enemy to be 'my ancient friend'. His lack of vindictiveness
differentiates him from his pupil, whose first act of self-assertion under
his tutelage is to beat her old nursemaid. Later he is horrified to discover
that Cleopatra has ordered the killing of one of his prisoners, which he
sees as a breach of hospitality. As Cleopatra says, 'he has no hatred in
him: he makes friends with everyone as he does with dogs and children'.
He arouses genuine affection in his officers and personal slaves, who are
frequently exasperated by his neglect of his own welfare. In contrast with
Shakespeare's Caesar, only very rarely does he refer to himself in the
third person, as when he declares, 'Caesar, in good or bad fortune, looks
his fate in the face'. Those around him, especially his adolescent charge,
whom he invariably treats with affectionate indulgence, are his moral and
intellectual inferiors.[31]

2. Caesar in Song

Of the twenty-plus operas that have been written about Caesar, the
most famous is Frederick Handel's *Giulio Cesare in Egitto* (first
performed at the Haymarket, London, in 1724) with libretto by Nicola
Francesco Haym. It comprises a passionate love story, a failed Egyptian-
based conspiracy against Caesar's life, a thwarted suicide attempt on
Cleopatra's part, and a complicated sub-plot involving Pompey's widow
Cornelia who is the object of attention from several wooers.

When the curtain rises, Caesar, sung by a contralto (!), is being
acclaimed victor by a chorus of Egyptians. After being shown Pompey's
head, he ponders sorrowfully upon the mutability of fortune: 'Soul of

[a] William Warren in Cecil B. de Mille's *Cleopatra*

[b] Louis Cahern as Caesar in Joseph L. Mankiewicz's *Julius Caesar*

Plate ix

Plate x.   Claude Rains in Gabriel Pascal's *Caesar and Cleopatra*

great Pompey…your triumphs were but a shadow, your greatness was but a shadow and you yourself are but a shadow'. Cleopatra decides to seduce him in order to win his support against her brother Tolomeo. To test the waters without revealing her royal identity, she disguises herself as a slave. Caesar falls for her charms, which causes her to reflect, 'A pretty woman can do anything if she opens her mouth or turns her eyes in amorous manner'. Cleopatra is equally stricken by Caesar and decides to make moves on 'the man who has stolen my heart as a prisoner of love'. And so it goes on. When Caesar learns of the conspiracy to murder him, he bravely declares that 'Caesar has never known fear'. A moment later he flees for his life. A battle ensues, which leads to the capture of Cleopatra. Just as she is about to commit suicide Caesar arrives to rescue her. 'Are you Caesar or his ghost?', she inquires, anticipating events to come at Philippi. Caesar bestows upon her the crown of Egypt and she in return promises to worship him as the emperor of Rome. The opera ends in a universal celebration of peace, with the lovers swearing to be faithful for all time. Daft as it may seem thus baldly summarised, the plot of *Guilio Cesare* explores, not without subtlety, the perennial tension between public duty and private desire that is experienced by those who are born to high estate. Through the seductive charms of Cleopatra, it also trumpets the power of sex.

3. Caesar on Celluloid

Caesar's first appearance on screen was in *Giulio Cesare* (1914), a semi-documentary starring Amleto Novelli which covers the period from his marriage to his first wife Cornelia to his assassination. Shakespeare's play has been filmed at least three times, first by David Bradley in 1951 and most recently by Stuart Burge in 1969. The most memorable of these is Joseph L. Mankiewicz's 1953 black and white version for MGM, a highly distinguished example of *film noir*. As in Fritz Lang's classic film *Metropolis*, urban decay, exemplified here by streets littered with refuse and walls daubed with graffiti, speaks to the moral corruption of the times. Mankiewicz was the first director to convey on camera the Rome of dark alleys and rickety tenements. To suggest the shadowy motives of victim and conspirators alike, he shot many of the scenes in shadow. Caesar (played by Louis Cahern), rather than suggesting a once-great-man in his decline, exudes an effete seediness that is somewhat reminiscent of the crooks who appear in gangster movies set in Chicago at the time of the Prohibition (pl. ix, b).[32]

Shaw's *Caesar and Cleopatra*, shot partly on location in Egypt by Gabriel Pascal in 1946, was derided at the time as 'the biggest financial disaster in the history of British cinema'. Claude Rains is certainly the oddest Caesar on celluloid (pl. x). Described by one critic as 'an utterly negative and phantom Caesar', he is low-key, softly spoken and faintly epicene. In his relationship with Cleopatra he cultivates the avuncular to excess. Far from being a man of action, this is a Caesar who could not even say 'boo' to his own ghost. Even Rains' body type – short, podgy and flat-footed – counts heavily against him. For all his shortcomings, however, he projects the acceptable face of Roman, and, by extension, British imperialism at the end of World War II – endowed with inexhaustible reserves of sweet reasonableness to counter every provocation.

Caesar has also featured in several Hollywood blockbusters. The Caesar of Cecil B. DeMille's *Cleopatra* (1934) played by William Warren is notable for his complete imperviousness to the seductive charms of Claudette Colbert's Cleopatra (pl. ix, a). 'Can't you see I'm busy?', he barks impatiently, as the queen vainly seeks to gain his attention by twisting curvaceously across his line of vision. She eventually succeeds by appealing to his lust for gold, which she arouses by reports of India's wealth. 'Pretty girl...charming...now what do you know about India?' he mumbles with all the passion of a gourmet contemplating an after-dinner mint. We need hardly doubt that Cleopatra is equally impervious to Caesar's animal magic. 'This is no time to talk of Romans. I haven't had breakfast. I'm hungry', is her retort to her tutor at the beginning of the film, when he informs her that Caesar has arrived in Alexandria. A moment later she inquires slyly, 'What age did you say this Caesar is?'.

The first half of Joseph L. Mankiewicz's *Cleopatra* (1963), which deals with the domestication of Caesar (Rex Harrison) at the hands of Cleopatra (Elizabeth Taylor), might aptly have been called 'Caesar in Love', were it not for the fact that Harrison and his co-star conspicuously fail to generate much body heat (pl. xi, a and xii). Harrison's early lines owe much to Shaw's Caesar. His angry outburst, 'Have you broken out of your nursery to irritate the adults?... You are what I say you are, and nothing more', could have come straight from Shaw. Arguably the most convincing Caesar in the filmic canon, Harrison is articulate, urbane, witty and shrewd. Without any posturing whatsoever, he radiates a quiet authority. At the same time, he reveals a vulnerable side to Caesar's character, manifested by his grief at Pompey's death, his fits of epilepsy, his childlessness, and his belief that his efforts on behalf of Rome go largely unappreciated. As the film progresses he increasingly falls under the spell of Cleopatra, who understands his weaknesses and compensates for them by providing him with an heir. Caesar as an

[a] Rex Harrison and Elizabeth Taylor in Joseph L. Mankiewicz's *Cleopatra*

[b] Asterix with Cleopatra in *Asterix and Cleopatra*

Plate xi.

Plate xii.   Rex Harrison in the carpet scene from Joseph L. Mankiewicz's
        Cleopatra

anxious father-to-be pacing the officers' mess prior to his son's birth is a nice touch, overlooked by ancient biographers. We cut to Rome and Cleopatra's entry – with 6000 extras, still one of the most costly scenes ever filmed. Caesar, showing signs of strain on account of the senate's ingratitude, describes himself as 'a humble man, anxious to serve', yet in the next breath reveals his desire to become emperor of Rome. He is driven to this last resort, we are made to believe, not from ambition, but from exhaustion. When he leaves for the senate on the ides of March, Cleopatra usurps the traditional role assigned to Calpurnia (as, she does, incidentally in Cecil B. DeMille's *Cleopatra*). Her parting words to him are, 'The world except for you is filled with little men'. In more ways than one, it is a fitting epitaph.

Stanley Kubrick's *Spartacus* (1960), which was hailed when first released as 'the thinking man's epic', provides a necessarily minor role for the then twenty-seven year old Caesar (played by John Gavin). However, Dalton Trumbo's well-researched script has the virtue of enabling Laurence Olivier as Crassus to interpret his role as if he were a kind of proto-Caesar, as in the scene where he angrily rejects the suggestion that he should march on Rome and assume the dictatorship. Much later, at the baths, Crassus cosies up to Caesar and seeks to woo him to the cause of the senatorial élite. 'Rome is the mob', Caesar observes naively. To which Crassus replies, 'No, Rome is an eternal thought in the mind of God'. This scene, with its delicate whiff of homoeroticism, offers an explanation not only for the *amicitia* between Caesar and Crassus but also for the factious divisions within the senate – no mean feat for a Hollywood epic.[33]

4. Caesar in Fiction

The Caesar novel, which is a phenomenon of the past eighty years or so, exhibits more variety in its depictions of the principal character – as well as more ingenuity in its plots – than do the works in any other medium. In Wallace Irwin's *The Julius Caesar Murder Case* (1935) a reporter for the *Evening Tiber* discovers how Julius Caesar, known as the Big Fella, faked his own assassination so that he could retire in safety from public life. Thornton Wilder's *The Ides of March* (1948) uses a wide selection of 'ancient sources' including Caesar's journal, his memoranda and his correspondence with friends and associates, to construct a complex picture of Caesar's personality as viewed from a variety of angles. Wilder also adopts a highly original chronological schema by having each of the four 'books' that comprise the narrative begin earlier than its predecessor. Bertolt Brecht's *The History of Julius Caesar: Fragment of a Novel* (1957) sees events through the eyes of Caesar's secretary. In *The Young Caesar* (1958) and *Imperial Caesar* (1960) Rex Warner has Caesar reflect upon his life at the moment of its ending. In Allan Massie's *Caesar* (1993) we view Caesar's final years through the eyes of the conspirator Decimus Brutus. Colleen McCullough's *Caesar's Women* (1996), *Let the Dice Fly* (1997) and *The October Horse* (2002) combine erudition with the type of racy prose that sells like hot cakes in airport terminals. 'Before the Roman Republic was his...her noblewomen were Caesar's greatest conquest', says the puff on the dust-jacket of the former. In Alice Borchardt's *Night of the Wolf* (1999) we follow the trail of an undercover female werewolf, whose assignment is to assassinate Caesar before he invades Britain. In Steven Saylor's *Rubicon* (1999) the detective Gordianus the finder investigates the death of Pompey's cousin against the background of the Civil War. Conn Iggulden's *Emperor: The Gates of Rome* (2003), the first in a projected trilogy, is a *Bildungsroman*, which offers a romanticised portrait of Caesar's early years. Comedy, intrigue and romance, seen through the eyes of reliable and unreliable narrators at various degrees of proximity to Caesar, continue to inform this light-hearted literary sub-genre.

Caesar appears in a subsidiary role in the popular series of French cartoon books (text by René Goscinny and drawings by Alberto Uderzo), some of which have now been filmed (pl. xi, b), tracing the fortunes of Asterix the Gaul. Is there here an echo of the name of Ambiorix, the Gallic chieftain who defeated Caesar's legions and evaded capture all his life? (p. 40). The action is set in a village in Brittany which is holding out indomitably after the rest of the country has been overrun. The year is 50 BCE. 'It is well known that Caesar had quite a bit of Gaul', we are told. Asterix and his plucky pals, though constantly squabbling among themselves, repeatedly triumph over the Romans and retain their independence 'thanks to magic, the protection of the gods, and low cunning'. Caesar is depicted as a gaunt, ageing, Roman-nosed commander with a six-foot *pilum* stuck up his back passage. The series may well owe some of its popularity to the fact that it offers a comical 'revisionist' interpretation of the Gallic conquest. More importantly, Asterix also exemplifies the courage displayed by the French resistance in the face of a brutal oppressor during the German occupation.

Caesar's continuing visibility in the media is due not only to his historical importance but also to the variety of guises which his character can be made to adopt. The popularity of Shakespeare's play, not to mention Caesar's association with some of the darkest chapters in twentieth-century history, those of a fascist orientation especially, have further guaranteed his prominence. Few historical figures can bear the weight of so many different interpretations, few can exemplify so many unresolved tensions within the human condition. In Caesar's life we read of the terrible isolation of absolute power, of the paradoxical contrast between autocracy and physical frailty, of the inevitable corruption that attends upon the fulfilment of man's highest aspirations, of the conflict between noble aims and dishonourable means, of the servant of the state caught between public duty and private desire, of the vanity and futility of ambition itself. The mood in which the treatments are cast may be tragical, historical, melodramatic, comical, farcical, satirical or romantic. Caesar is variously presented as the up-and-coming careerist, the paranoid tyrant, the architect of universal peace, the dreamer, the isolated autocrat, the star-struck lover, the rigid militarist, the detached pragmatist, the bloodthirsty man of action, the ageing yet still sexually vulnerable male of late-middle life.

There are as many Caesars in the media as we may discover in Caesar the man.

Notes

1. There was only a handful of Roman personal names in use. Those included in this narrative were abbreviated as follows: C. = Gaius; Cn. = Gnaeus; D. or Dec. = Decimus; L. = Lucius; M. = Marcus; P. = Publius; Serv. = Servius, Q. = Quintus; T. = Titus; Ti. = Tiberius.

2. It is impossible to give modern monetary equivalents of Roman coinage. However, it may help to bear in mind that in Caesar's day a legionary earned about four *denarii* per week. A golden *denarius* was worth 25 silver *denarii*. A silver *denarius*, the coin most frequently in use, was the equivalent of four sesterces. In short, 60,000 gold *denarii* was a fabulous sum of money.

3. The common citizenry wore a plain white toga, those of senatorial rank a white one with a broad purple edge.

4. Patricians constituted a class of Roman aristocrats who enjoyed special privileges. Their origin is unknown. In the early Republic they developed a monopoly over political office but this was increasingly challenged by the lower order known as the *plebs*.

5. A *cognomen*, which was usually hereditary, distinguished different families within the same *gens*. Many were in origin honorific.

6. As M.I. Finley (*Aspects of Antiquity* [Harmondsworth 1977] 126) observed, 'No great genius was needed to think up the idea of giving every girl a personal name, as was done with boys. It is as if the Romans wished to suggest very pointedly that women were not, or ought not to be, genuine individuals but only fractions of a family.'

7. The Romans collected taxes from their provinces by auctioning the right to do so to the highest bidders. Naturally the successful bidders expected to make a handsome profit from their investment, but on this occasion they had failed to break even.

8. For the chronology of Caesar's legislation passed during his consulship, see Seager (1979, Appendix 1).

9. The Helvetii, a tribe which inhabited modern-day Switzerland, have given their name to the *Confederatio Helvetica*, whose initials (CH) are used to indicate the provenance of Swiss motor vehicles.

10. The precise terminal date of Caesar's proconsulship is unknown. Indeed it is quite likely that no date was laid down in either of the laws

granting him his command. See Seager (1979, Appendix 2).

11. Perhaps Goethe got it right when he declared, 'we have become too humane not to be repelled by Caesar's triumphs' (quoted in Meier 1982, 16).

12. The memory of Cato's heroic gesture lives on in the choice of the name Utica for a city in upstate New York.

13. The rostra was so-named because the original structure had been adorned with *rostra* (prows) of enemy ships captured in the fourth century BCE. Under Caesar's supervision the old rostra, located in front of the *curia*, had been replaced with a new one that stood in a commanding position overlooking the forum and on an axis with it.

14. For the influence of Plato's thought on Brutus, see Sedley (1997, 41-53).

15. 'Ides' is a word of uncertain etymology. In the old, lunar calendar the ides were supposed to coincide with the full moon.

16. *Pace* Habicht (1990, 74 with n. 35).

17. The master of horses was second-in-command to the dictator and appointed directly by him. It is difficult to resist the conclusion that Caesar chose Lepidus in part because he was a man of very meagre ability though Welch ('The career of M. Aemilius Lepidus', in *Hermes* [123.4] 1995, 443-54) claims that he was useful because of his diplomatic skills.

18. Cicero (*on Divination* 2.23) claims that Caesar died 'in the presence of so many of his centurions'. Since centurions would not have been permitted inside the *curia*, he may be emphasising the pathos of Caesar's death for rhetorical effect. Alternatively he may be alluding to the fact that Caesar had recently granted senatorial status to some of his former centurions.

19. It is Shakespeare alone who, perhaps quoting from an unknown source, puts the famous words '*Et tu, Brute?*' into Caesar's mouth.

20. This is in line with the theory proposed by the forensic psychiatrist Dr. Harold Burstayn in the documentary 'Who Killed Julius Caesar?' Burstayn argues that Caesar, who was suffering from temporal lobe epilepsy, in effect took his own life by 'using the conspirators' agenda to serve his own agenda'.

21. The fact that the Julii had a tomb within the city walls is a strong indication of the prestige attaching to their family, since, because of sanitary requirements and fear of religious pollution, most burials took place outside. The site of the tomb is unknown.

22. A comparable modern analogy is the popular grief occasioned by Princess Diana's death, which, had her funeral taken place in a confined space such as the Roman forum with a vast crowd in attendance, might well have generated equal hysteria.

23. 75 *denarii* would have supported a low-income Roman family for almost two months.

24. See Weinstock (1971, 370-84) for discussion of the details surrounding the establishment of the cult.

25. Adoption was a very common practice in Rome, as elsewhere in the ancient world. According to traditional procedure, followed in this instance, the adopted son took his adoptive father's full name, appending to it the name of his own *gens* with the adjectival suffix *–ianus*.

26. For a full discussion of the comet, see Ramsey and Licht (1997).

27. Old soldiers have been favourably compared to Caesar. William Manchester's *American Caesar: General Douglas MacArthur* (Boston, 1978) points out parallels between Caesar and MacArthur in character, style of leadership, and career patterns.

28. 'Caesarism' took on a rather different connotation in twentieth-century political debate. A. Gramsci (*Selections from the Prison Notebooks*, ed. and trans. by Q. Hoare and G.N. Smith [London 1971] 219) defined it as follows: 'a situation in which the forces in conflict balance each other in such a way that a continuation of the conflict can only terminate in their reciprocal destruction'.

29. *The Philosophy of History* (1st edn 1831), trans. by J. Sibree (New York 1944) 313.

30. The translations are from the edition by D.A. Saunders and J.H. Collins, pp. 479 and 486 respectively.

31. Mention should also be made of Giovacchino Forzano's *Cesare* (1939), in which Mussolini is thought to have collaborated. When it learns of Caesar's death, the crowd becomes 'mad with tragic fury', as the stage direction reads. Intended to serve as a warning of the consequences of assassinating *Il Duce*, the play is highly indicative of his paranoia.

32. M. Wyke, 'Film style and fascism: *Julius Caesar* (1953)' (forthcoming in *Film Studies*), investigates the interesting political interpretations to which the film gave rise, both in its making and on release. She quotes its producer John Houseman as follows:

> While never deliberately exploiting the historical parallels, there were certain emotional patterns arising from political events of the immediate past that we were prepared to evoke – Hitler, Mussolini and Ciano at the Brenner Pass.

As Wyke notes, the film is ambivalent in its representation of fascism, depicting both its attractions and its dangers.

33. The latest attempt to revive Caesar's ghost is an American mini-series by the DeAngelis Group entitled *Julius Caesar* (2003), directed by Uli Edel and starring Jeremy Sisto as Caesar.

Further Reading

1. Ancient Sources in Translation

Caesar: *Civil War* (1997), trans. with introduction and notes by J.M. Carter (Oxford and New York).

Caesar: *Gallic War* (1996), trans. with introduction and notes by C. Hammond (Oxford and New York).

Cicero: *Letters to Atticus* (1978), trans. with introduction by D.R. Shackleton Bailey (Harmondsworth).

Cicero: *Letters to Friends* (1978) 2 vols., trans. with introduction by D.R. Shackleton Bailey (Harmondsworth).

Dio: *Roman History*, 9 vols., Loeb Classical Library (Cambridge, MA).

Lucan: *Civil War* (1992), trans. with introduction and notes by S.H. Braund (Oxford and New York).

Plutarch: *Fall of the Roman Republic* (1972), trans. by R. Warner, revised with introduction by R. Seager (Harmondsworth).

Suetonius: *Lives of the Twelve Caesars* (1979), trans. by R. Graves, revised with introduction by M. Grant (Harmondsworth).

2. Discussion of Sources

Lamberton, R. (2001): *Plutarch* (London and New Haven).

Pelling, C.B.R. (2002): *Plutarch and History* (London and Swansea), esp. ch. 11.

Wallace-Hadrill, A. (1983): *Suetonius: the Scholar and his Critics* (London and New Haven).

3. Modern Biographies

Badian, E. (1996): 'Iulius Caesar, Gaius', in *Oxford Classical Dictionary*, 3rd edn., edd. S. Hornblower and A. Spawforth (Oxford), 780-2.

Balsdon, J.P.V.D. (1967): *Julius Caesar and Rome* (London) [somewhat old fashioned in approach but highly readable].

Bradford, E. (1984): *Julius Caesar: the Pursuit of Power* (New York).

Gelzer, M. (1969): *Caesar: Politician and Statesman*, trans. of the 6th German edn. (1959), first published in 1921 (Oxford) [an excellent scholarly investigation].

Grant, M. (1974): *Caesar* (London) [well-illustrated with much useful background information].

Meier, C. (1982): *Caesar: a Biography*, trans. by D. McLintock (New York) [detailed but designed for the general reader and a first-class read].

Southern, P. (2001): *Julius Caesar* (Stroud, etc.).

Weinstock, S. (1971): *Divus Julius* (Oxford) [a scholarly investigation of the thorny question as to which honours were awarded to Caesar in his lifetime].

Yavetz, Z. (1983): *Julius Caesar and his Public Image* (London and Ithaca) [on Caesar's involvement with the Roman *plebs*].

4. Background Studies

Beard, M. and Crawford, M. (1985): *Rome in the Late Republic Problems and Interpretations* (London).

Meyer, E. (1922): *Caesars Monarchie und das Prinzipat des Pompeius*, 3rd edn (Stuttgart and Berlin).

Mommsen, T. (1958): *The History of Rome*, originally published in Berlin (1856-85) as *Römische Geschichte*, trans. by D.A. Saunders and J.H. Collins [a gripping account, even though Mommsen is hugely biased in favour of Caesar].

Seager, R. (1979): *Pompey: A Political Biography* (Oxford, Berkeley and Los Angeles).

Syme, R. (1939): *The Roman Revolution* (Oxford) [though mostly concerned with Octavian's rise to power, this has an extremely useful chapter entitled 'Caesar the Dictator'].

5. The Gallic Wars and Invasion of Britain

Barlow, J., etc. (1998): *Julius Caesar as an Artful Reporter: The War Commentaries as a Political Instrument* (London).

Ellis, P.B. (1980): *Caesar's Invasion of Britain* (New York).

Ramon, J. (2001): *Caesar Against the Celts* (New Jersey).

6. Cicero and Caesar

Everitt, A. (2002): *Cicero: The Life and Times of Rome's Greatest Politician* (New York) [highly readable account of Cicero's reflections on Roman life and politics].

Gotoff, H.C. (1993): *Cicero's Caesarian Speeches: A Stylistic Commentary* (London and Chapel Hill).

Habicht, Chr. (1990): *Cicero: The Politician* (Baltimore).

7. The Ides of March

Balsdon, J.P.V.D. (1958): 'The Ides of March', in *Historia* 7, 80-94.

Collins, J.H. (1955): 'Caesar and the corruption of power', in *Historia* 4, 445-65.

Ehrenberg, V. (1964): 'Caesar's final aims', in *Harvard Studies in Classical Philology* 68, 149-61.

Horsfall, N. (1974): 'The Ides of March: some new problems', in *Greece & Rome* 21, 191-9 [excellent detail on the order of events on the final day].

Lewis, N. (1985): *The Ides of March* (Toronto) [very useful source book for the murder].

Sedley, D. (1997): 'The ethics of Brutus and Cassius', in *Journal of Roman Studies* 87, 41-53.

Smith, R.E. (1957): 'The conspiracy and the conspirators', in *Greece & Rome* 4, 58-70.

Schmitthener, W. (1962): 'Das Attentat auf Caesar am 15 März 44 v. Chr.', in *Geschichte in Wissenschaft und Unterricht* 11, 685-95.

Storch, R.H. (1995): 'Relative deprivation and the Ides of March', in *Ancient History Bulletin* 9 (1) 45-52.

Yavetz, Z. (1974): 'Existimatio, fama, and the Ides of March', in *Harvard Studies in Classical Philology* 78, 35-65.

8. The Avenger

Ramsey, J.T. and Licht, A.L. (1997): *The Comet of 44 BC and Caesar's Funeral Games* (Atlanta).

Tarn, W.W. and Charlesworth, M.P. (1965): *Octavian, Antony and Cleopatra* (Cambridge).

9. Art and Archaeology

Toynbee, J.M.C (1978): *Roman Historical Portraits* (Ithaca and London) [a good discussion of the portraits and literary descriptions of leading late-republican figures].

Claridge, A. (1998): *Rome* (Oxford) [the best guidebook for anyone interested in retracing Caesar's steps in Rome – literally].

10. Caesar's Legacy and Reception

C. Hammond's 'Caesar's Influence', xxxvi-xliii in her Introduction to *The Gallic War* (Oxford 1996), and M. Grant, ch. 8 in *Caesar* (London 1974) provide a solid starting point. F. Gundolf's *The Mantle of Caesar* (trans. by J.W. Hartmann, London 1929) is adulatory. P. Baehr, *Caesar and the Fading of the Roman World* (New Brunswick 1998) examines the phenomenon of 'Caesarism' in the nineteenth century as exemplified by the reign of Napoleon III. R. Chevallier's *Présence de César: Hommages au doyen M. Rambaud* (Paris 1985) contains articles on Caesar's legacy. C. Edwards, *Roman Presences: Receptions of Rome in European Culture* (Oxford 1998) includes discussion of the origins of fascism. For Caesar's influence on Mussolini, see J. Whittam, *Fascist Italy* (Manchester 1995); R. Visser, 'Fascist doctrine and the cult of the Romanità', in *Journal of Contemporary History* 27.1, 5-22; and M. Wyke, 'Sawdust Caesar: Mussolini, Julius Caesar, and the drama of dictatorship', 167-85 in M. Wyke and M. Biddiss, eds, *The Uses and Abuse of Antiquity* (Bern, etc. 1999).

11. Caesar in the Media

For Lucan, see W.R. Johnson, *Momentary Monsters: Lucan and his Heroes* (Ithaca and London 1978). G.B. Harrison, *Julius Caesar in Shakespeare, Shaw and the Ancients* (New York 1960), has a useful introduction. For the origins of Shakespeare's play, see S.T. Sohmer, *Shakespeare's Invention of Julius Caesar* (London 1995). H. Bloom, ed., *Julius Caesar* (New York 1998) offers several interpretations. For stagings, see A. Humphreys, 'The play in performance', in *Shakespeare: Julius Caesar* (Oxford 1994) 48-72; and B. Sylvan, 'Julius Caesar on stage and screen' in *Shakespeare: Julius Caesar* (New York, 1987). M. Holroyd, *Bernard Shaw: The One-Volume Definitive Edition* (London and New York 1997), provides a short discussion of Shaw's fascination with Caesar. For critical discussion, see J. Bartolini, 'Shaw's ironic view of Caesar', in *Twentieth Century Literature: a Scholarly and Critical Journal* 27.4 (1981) 331-42; E. Wilson, *Shaw on Shakespeare* (New York 2002). J. Solomon, *The Ancient World in the Cinema* (London and New Haven, 2001) includes a useful discussion of Caesar in film (pp. 58-78).

12. Other Media

DVD/Video, 'Who Killed Julius Caesar?', a television documentary by Atlantic Productions, for which the author acted as historical consultant, is available. To order, telephone +44(0)238 024 8760.

Index

aedileship 16, 27 f.

Ahenobarbus, L. Domitius 39

Alesia, siege of 42 f.

Alexander the Great 10, 27

Alexandria 49 f.

Ambiorix, Gallic chieftain 40 f.

amicitia (political alliance) 32, 41

Anna Perenna, festival of 72

Antistius, physician 76

Antony, Mark 45, 48, 59-61, 64, 73, 75-7, 81, 83, 88, 90, 92

Appian, Greek historian of Rome (1st – 2nd cent. CE) 11

Aquila, Pontius, assassin 58, 66, 91

Artemidorus, friend of Caesar 76

Arverni, Gallic tribe 42

assemblies, *see comitia*

Asterix, imaginary Gallic warrior 112

Atia, Caesar's grand-niece, mother of C. Octavius 24

Augustus, *see* Octavius, C.

Balbus, L. Cornelius, Caesar's agent 38, 56, 60

Bibulus, M., Caesar's consular colleague 20, 28, 32

bona dea, festival in honour of 31

Brennus, Gallic chieftain 35

Britain, Caesar's invasion of 9, 39 f.

Brutus, Dec., assassin 52, 59, 65, 72 f., 90 f.

Brutus, M., assassin 49, 63-9, 75-7, 81, 88, 91, 101

Caesar, C. Julius, Caesar's father 23

Caesar, C. Julius,
    celeritas (rapidity of movement) 2
    clementia (clemency) 5, 48 f., 51, 60

dignitas (concern for personal worth) 97 f., 102
    fits of epilepsy 1, 57 f.
    generalship 2, 48
    portents, distrustful of 3
    sexuality 1 f.

Caesarion, Ptolemy XV Caesar 50, 54 f., 92

Caesarism 97 f., 102

calendar, Gregorian 96

calendar, Julian 56, 95

Calpurnia, Caesar's third wife 2, 33, 41, 54 f., 92

campus Martius (Field of Mars) 52, 54, 82

Capitol 52, 77

Carrhae, battle of 41, 45

Cassius, C., assassin 49, 63-5, 67, 72, 75, 77, 81, 88, 91, 101

Casivellaunus, British chieftain 40

Catilinarian conspiracy 9

Catiline, L. Sergius Catilina, politician 20, 29

Cato, M. Porcius, politician 2, 5, 30 f., 51, 64, 101

Celts 36, 38

Cicero, M. Tullius, orator 5, 9, 14, 29 f., 41, 48, 51, 58, 66 f.

Cincinnatus, dictator 17

Cinna, L. Cornelius, praetor 77, 81

Cinna, Helvius, victim of mistaken identity 84

Civil War 45-56

Cleopatra VII Philopator 2, 50, 54 f., 62, 68, 92

cognomen (name often awarded as an honorific) 23, 59

coinage 35, 115

comet 89
comitia centuriata (centuriate
assembly) 19, 59, 62
comitia tributa (tribal
assembly) 19, 58
Commentaries, Caesar's 7-9, 38,
48, 97
consulship 14, 17, 31 f., 41, 55,
58 f.
Cornelia, Caesar's first wife 2,
24, 26
corona civica (civic crown,
awarded for valour on the
field of battle) 25
Cossutia, Caesar's fiancée 24
Crassus, M. Licinius, politician
and financier 14, 26 f., 29,
31-3, 39, 41
curia (senate house) 41, 67, 74 f.,
84, 92
Curio, C Scribonius, tribune of the
plebs 1, 42, 45 f., 49, 101
cursus honorum (ladder of
offices) 16f.

Dante 101
deification 60, 73, 89, 91
dictatorship 5, 17, 27, 55 f., 60
Dio, Cassius, historian (*ca* 163-*ca*
235 CE) 11
Dolabella, P. Cornelius,
consul 25, 59, 88, 91
domus publica (lit. 'state house'),
residence of *pontifex
maximus* 29, 73 f.
Dyrrhachium, Caesar's siege of
Pompey at 49

fasces (bundles of axes and rods
carried by *lictors*) 58, 82

Gallic War 35-43
Gallia Narbonensis (Narbonese
Gaul), *see provincia*
gens (clan) 23

Gergovia, Caesar's defeat at 42
Germans 36, 42
gladiatorial contests 27, 54, 67,
83, 96
gloria (military glory) 17 f.
governorships, *see* proconsulship,
propraetorship
Gracchus, T. Sempronius, tribune
of the *plebs* 14, 20

Helvetii, German tribe 38 f.
Hirtius, Aulus 8, 59, 90
homosexuality, Roman attitudes
towards 25

Jews 50, 56, 84, 97
Juba I, king of Numidia 49, 51,
54
Julia, Caesar's aunt 24, 26
Julia, Caesar's daughter 6, 33, 40 f.,
54, 82
Julian Forum 4, 56
July 60, 95

Kingship 7, 13, 27, 59, 61, 92

Labienus, Q. Atius, Caesar's
legate 8
Latin festival 59
legati (legates) 8, 36
Lepidus, M. 48, 72, 76, 81, 92
lictor (official who carried the
fasces as symbol of a
magistrate's authority) 58,
82
Lucan 10, 100
lupercalia (festival) 61

Marius, C., military general,
consul and Caesar's uncle by
marriage 14, 18, 24, 26
Mattius, C., friend of Caesar 99
Maximus, Q. Fabius, appointed
consul by Caesar 58
Maximus, Q. Fabius, dictator 17

military tribunes 26, 36
Milo, T. Annius, defended by
    Cicero 20, 41
Mithridates, king of Pontus 18, 25 f.
Munda, battle of 55
Mussolini, Benito 85, 98, 117,
    122
Mutina, siege of 90

Napoleon Bonaparte 98
Nervii, Gallic tribe 38 f., 40 f.
Nicolaus of Damascus, Greek
    writer (born *ca* 64 BCE) 9
Nicomedes, king of Bithynia 2,
    25
novi homines ('new men' of
    senatorial rank) 14

Octavius, C., future emperor
    Augustus 7, 9, 24, 51, 62,
    85, 87-93
Oppius, C., agent and biographer
    of Caesar 10, 38, 50, 56
optimates (politicians who sought
    to preserve the *status
    quo*) 23
Ovid 100

Pansa, C., consul 59, 90
Parthia 45, 55, 59, 61, 63, 68
Paterculus, Velleius, Roman
    historian 10
paterfamilias (head of the
    family) 24
patricians 16, 23, 25
Pharnaces II, king of Pontus 50
Pharsalus, battle of 49
Philippi, battle of 91
Piso, L. Calpurnius, politician and
    Caesar's father-in-law 33,
    78, 82, 92
plebs (the common people) 14,
    16, 23, 28 f., 88, 96
Pliny the Elder, Latin scholar and
    writer (23-79 CE) 10

Plutarch, Greek biographer (*ca*
    50-120 CE) 10 f.
Pollio, C. Asinius, Roman
    politician and historian (76
    BCE-4 CE) 10, 32, 46
Pompeia, Caesar's second wife 2,
    27, 31
Pompeius, Sextus, son of Pompey
    the Great 55, 91
Pompey the Great, Gn. Pompeius
    Magnus 4, 14, 17 f., 27, 31-3,
    39, 41, 45-9
pontifex maximus (supreme
    pontiff or senior religious
    official) 3, 19, 28 f., 60
populares (politicians who
    exploited the needs of the
    populace) 23
Porcia, wife of M. Brutus 64, 74,
    92
praetorship 16, 30, 88
proconsulship, propraetorship 17 f.,
    31, 35-43
proscriptions 13, 26, 31, 91
provincia 36
Provence, *see provincia*
Ptolemy XIII 49 f.
Ptolemy XIV 50, 54
Ptolemy XV Caesar, *see* Caesarion
Pulcher, P. Clodius, politician 16,
    20, 31, 41

quaestorship 16, 26

Rebilus, C. Caninius, consul for
    one day 59
regia (lit. 'palace', building in
    the forum where *pontifex
    maximus* had his office) 29
religion 19 f.
Rome, conditions in 20 f.
rostra (speaker's platform) 61,
    82 f.
Rubicon, river 46

Sallust, Roman historian (86-34 BCE) 9
senate 14, 62
senatus consultum ultimum (last decree of the senate) 14, 46, 48
Servilia, mother of M. Brutus 2, 30, 64, 88 f., 91
Shakespeare 105-8
Shaw, G. B. 107 f., 109.
Spartacus, leader of slave revolt 26
Spurinna, seer 62, 74
stoic philosophy 51
Suetonius, Roman biographer (*ca* 69-*ca* 140 CE) 2, 10 f.
Sulla, L. Cornelius, military general and dictator 2, 5, 13-18, 24 f., 60
supplicatio (thanksgiving for military victory) 39 f.
supreme pontiff, *see pontifex maximus*

Tarquinius Superbus, last king of Rome 13
taxation 19
Thapsus, battle of 51
theatre of Pompey 72 f., 92
toga, Roman citizen's dress 3, 23
Trebonius, C., assassin 58, 75, 91
tribuni plebis (tribunes of the people) 14, 23, 38, 58 f., 87
triumph 17 f., 31, 52-4, 58
triumvirate, so-called 'first 10, 32
triumvirate, so-called 'second' 32, 90 f.

Utica, siege of 51

Venus Genetrix 54, 60, 83, 89, 93
Vercingetorix, Gallic chieftain 38, 42, 53 f.
Verres, C., governor of Sicily (73-71 BCE) 17

Vestal virgins 29, 31
Voltaire 106

will, Caesar's 51, 78, 81

Zela, battle of 50